Motion Before Motivation

The Success Secret
That Never Fails

Michael "Mike D." Dolpies

Printed in the U.S.A.

Published By: Ocean View Publishing, LLC

Dolpies, Michael J. 1979-
Motion Before Motivation, The Success Secret That Never Fails

Success, Self-Help, Business
ISBN-10: 0-9799104-0-4
ISBN-13: 9780979910401

Disclaimer:
The purpose of this book is to educate and entertain. The author and publisher does not guarantee that anyone following the techniques, suggestions, ideas and strategies will become successful. The author and publisher shall have neither, liability nor responsibility to anyone with respect to any loss or damage caused, or alleged to be caused, directly or indirectly by the information contained in this book.

"Practical advice to help you reach your goals!"
    -Peggy McColl, New York Times Best-Selling Author

"This book will inspire you to overcome any obstacle that stands between you and the life you want and deserve."
    -Brian Tracy, President: Brian Tracy International

"Mike's like a young Earl Nightingale."
    -Ben Gay, III, "The Closers"

"Embrace the concepts in this book and start making things happen in your life!"
    -Tony Rubleski, Author of the "Mind Capture" Series

"The tools and inspiration to design the life you want, faster than you've ever dreamed possible."
    -Carol Frank, Birds Eye Consulting

Contents

Foreword

by John Graden

The Key Skill for Success

As a World Champion United States Kickboxing Team fighter and coach, I have competed on three continents. As a business owner I generated sales and profits over $30 million in a decade. In my experience, there is one key element to success that separates the best of us from the rest of us. You can read all the books (certainly read mine), take all the courses, and obtain all the degrees in the world, but unless you pull the trigger it will mean nothing.

Nothing happens until you get in motion. Indeed, many people make the mistake of thinking, "I'll get going once I get motivated." That is backwards. Motion leads to motivation, which is the theme of Mike's book. Mike is a great example of motion leading to motivation. He is a fast learner, but more importantly he quickly implements what he learns. That's the key skill to success and I'm confident this book will help you to pull the trigger on your next project.

This book will help you to create the life you want. It can be an inspiration and an illustration that you can live the life of your dreams no matter the obstacles.

Enjoy!

John Graden
Author, "The Impostor Syndrome"

www.JohnGraden.com

Acknowledgments

This book is dedicated to Julia and Marissa, my two little princesses. You are the reason I stay in motion.

To my wife - thank you for putting up with me. To my parents for laying a great foundation while giving me the freedom to develop self-trust.

To my colleague and friend who I got to know in tough times, Brett Lechtenberg, It is an honor to know you. To my clients - you are all much appreciated and you know it. To Ben Gay, III - you told me I could do it. To Elsa, my business partner, thanks for entertaining my seemingly endless flow of ideas – most of them goofy!

A special thanks to all authors, information marketers and speakers who I highly respect. I have interviewed some of you and have been studying the rest of you from a distance for a long time. I thank you all for the contributions you have made to my life. You have all taught me something of tremendous value! I'm sure I left some out. You too are appreciated!

A special thanks goes out to a few of my

favorites: Brian Tracy, Dan Kennedy, Tom Hopkins, Zig Ziglar, Anthony Robbins, Robert Cialdini, PH.D, Joe

Sugarman, Carol Frank, Peggy McColl, Robert Ringer,

Larry Winget, Joe Girard, Jack Canfield, Mark Victor

Hansen, Brendon Bouchard, Yanik Silver, Paul Hartunian, Steve Harrison, Warren Greshes, Daniel Levis, David Garfinkel, Joe Vitale, Kevin Hogan, Kenrick Cleveland, Napoleon Hill, Bill Glazier and Dave Frees. This list is really long because I'm always learning, so I'll stop here.

Preface

The Missing Link To Success

For years we have been told how important motivation is. I couldn't agree more! Motivation is extremely important. Unfortunately, many who have read and heard the motivational words don't bother to dig a little deeper. The kind of motivation you get at a pep rally or a seminar is only short-term; it does not last! Here's why...

The "rah-rah" full-of-hype, carrot and stick, external motivation is only made up of temporary feelings. Once those feelings wear off and you get back to reality, the motivation and inspiration drop like a thermometer on a cold day. You're left wondering, "where is it?" The truth is it was totally synthetic.

You and I live in the real world. And in the real world there are people and there are circumstances that aren't always so inspiring. The real world doesn't always make us "feel good." It is not always cooperative of our wishes for pressing forward to reach our goals. In fact, the real world can make us "feel" like giving up if we are not careful.

It is so important to understand real, authentic motivation is a by-product of getting in motion. It's
the kind of motivation that you can count on every day! It has its roots in taking consistent action.

Motivation is what comes after you get started. You'll never be motivated to reach your goals. You will only become motivated once you decide to get in motion toward reaching your goals.

As Harvard physiologist, Jerome Bruner said years ago: "You're more likely to act yourself into feeling, than feel yourself into acting."

In this book, you'll uncover proven gems, simple concepts and little secrets that will assist you (notice I did not say motivate you) in creating the life you want as quickly as you possibly can. Use this book to break down obstacles, to get ideas and remind yourself to "keep moving."

I appreciate the opportunity to be part of your life and do hope that you'll invest the short time it will take to finish this book. To paraphrase one of my favorite authors/mentors, Brian Tracy, just one key piece of information or advice given to you at the right time can save you from years of hard work and frustration. Your time is now – this is the Success Secret That Never Fails. Now take action, read and then apply!

Introduction

"The ancestor of every action is a thought"
(Emerson)

The morning it dawned on me that motion comes before motivation was a normal day like any other. I was listening to a "motivational" CD as I made the drive back home from dropping the little ones off at pre-school to begin work for the day. In a moment, I had a blinding flash of the obvious. Everything that was ever accomplished was a result of someone getting in motion, of taking action. The fact that you or someone else decides to get in "motion" is the same reason you enjoy much of what you have today. On the contrary, if you are not happy with your current situation, it is the result of remaining motionless in the quest of what you really want.

Getting started even when the timing is not right is one major key to success. And the best part is even if you mess up, you're really not failing.

But what if you made a "move" and it didn't work out? How do you explain that? I have

made many moves throughout my life that did not work out. I'm
sure I'll make more! Success is achieved by making new moves when the first set of moves doesn't work out. Failure is caused by repeating the same situation that does not work or by giving up altogether.

Common sense, which is defined as having an experience and then applying the experience to subsequent situations, will prevent you from repeating the same flawed motions. Let me give you an example.

After selling a very profitable business I had operated since I was just eighteen years old, I got involved in a very UN-profitable business relationship. When I speak to live audiences and relate this story I tell them to feel free to play the "crash and burn" sound effects! The relationship was totally one-sided. My "partners" did not do what they were obligated to do by contract. Fortunately, the default on their end made it easy for a few others and I to terminate the relationship. There were five of us altogether. Three of us, myself included, had lost well over six figures and almost two years of our lives.

We realized we needed to get in motion quickly to get out of this relationship before it meant the business demise of us all. So we got in motion and got out of the troubled relationship. With badly bruised wallets, but a renewed sense of motivation for what was possible now that we got this monkey off of our backs. Our new lives began and all of us went our separate ways and on to bigger and better things.

There are two lessons here.

One: The renewed motivation came after we got in motion and got out of the relationship. We recognized we made a bad move and acted boldly in our own best interest to correct the situation and move in a new direction. None of us considered the experience a failure because of the valuable wisdom we picked up along the way. Personally, I knew a higher power needed me to acquire the wisdom before I turned thirty!

Two: As you go through the rest of this book remember that it is getting in motion and making things happen that will bring you the joy, happiness and prosperity that you seek. Muster the courage to stay in motion but don't be afraid to change course if necessary. Motivation will come as a result of the energy generated by setting things in motion.

In Dog Years

Many people thought that I was crazy to think that, at my age, I could write a book on success. When the first printing of this book came out I was just twenty-nine years old. Most of my clients were older than me at the time. Most of my audiences were made up of people who had a few years on me. I have aged in "dog years" because I have acquired enough knowledge and real life experiences to compile this message when I was still pretty young. I have dealt with thousands of people one-on-one and in group settings. I have always been fascinated by what makes other people tick. I am enormously curious about life. I love people, no matter how flaky, cutthroat or sinister they can be at times.

How to Get Wise

Once I had an employee who was new to the industry we were working in. My mind was open to his ideas and enthusiasm for sure. But there were many occasions I had to explain to him why some of his particular ideas had no merit. Mainly because I used the idea in some way years prior and since that time discovered even better methods. In addition, I was not only an expert in the particular industry but a student as well. Always remember that wisdom comes through accumulated study and application of what you've learned.

I have read a great deal of books, and have done a great deal of research of numerous other programs on success. Beyond just giving you the philosophy and practical application of "Motion before Motivation," I have also sprinkled "evergreen" success principles throughout this book. The word "evergreen" means the principles are true now, were true 100 years ago, and will always be true.

Let's get in motion, shall we?

Chapter 1

There Are Three Kinds Of People In This World

"Eliminate the time between the idea and the act, and your dreams will become realities" (Edward Kramer)

1) Those who make things happen.

2) Those who watch what happens.

3) And those who stand around and wonder, "What happened?"

I learned about the three kinds of people from Bob Alexander when I was twenty years old. You are in control of what happens to you. Even if you trust in a higher power to guide you, you know that the higher power helps those who decide to help themselves. It is very rare that anyone on this planet will always be there to save you every single time you need help.

Assume that you are the only one (on this planet) who cares about your success and then act accordingly by making things happen in your life. Making things happen requires that you get and stay in motion toward your goals.

If someone does help you or you get that lucky break, consider it a bonus. And when it comes to luck, you must remember that luck is generated when action is cross-timed with preparation. Very often, it is just a matter of being in the right place, and being in the right place is a by-product of being in motion. As Dan Kennedy says, "Be somebody and be somewhere." Sometimes the "somewhere" is more important than the "somebody" at first.

As you make things happen for yourself you'll benefit everyone close to you. This is enough to drive most people. Since you are reading this book, it is no surprise to say that you belong to the first kind of people - the kind that makes things happen!

Ask yourself: "Am I taking some action and getting in motion at least a little bit every day?"

Don't be afraid to ask yourself questions. Don't be afraid to answer those questions. Only be afraid if you catch yourself saying... "Whaaatt?" to the answers!

Chapter 2

Newton's Three Laws
How This Success Secret Is
Scientifically Proven

"Our duty as men is to proceed as if limits to our ability did not exist" (Pierre Teilhard De Chardin)

Newton's First Law

An object at rest will remain at rest unless acted on by an unbalanced force. An object in motion continues in motion with the same speed and in the same direction unless acted upon by an unbalanced force.

This law is often called "The Law of Inertia."

There is a natural tendency for objects to keep on doing what they're doing. All objects resist changes in their state of motion. In the absence of an unbalanced force, an object in motion will maintain this state of motion.

Have you ever wondered why people who are successful often stay successful? Ever wondered why bad luck and misfortune seem to follow the same people? Let Newton's first law enlighten you as to why this is the case.

Here's the big truth about Motion Before Motivation...

You need to be sure that the actions you're taking are in the direction of clearly defined goals. If not, 'Natural Tendency" will work against you! Further, you have to be sure those actions are based on principles of success.

In human terms, the "Natural Tendency" is the force of habit. If someone is in the habit of constantly remaining in motion toward their goals, they will continue in that direction and get closer to them every day. If someone is in the habit of putting things off or waiting for the inspiration or motivation to compel them to get moving, then nothing will happen and they will remain "at rest." Of course, if you're going in the wrong direction, this scientific law will work against you too! Consider this my "disclaimer!"

Don't Wait Around, Get Going

There are cobweb-covered skeletons hanging around in the success waiting room. You definitely do not want to become one of them.

Keep Your Mind Open Because You Never Know Where Your Next "Kick In The Pants" Will Come From

As we go through our journey, you'll discover how to easily get yourself moving toward any goal that you want to achieve. But right now I want to gently
remind you of how important is to keep your mind open. Just one thing said by just one person at the right time can lead you to your next big "aha" moment. Here's an example.

I started my first business just six months out of high school. If you would've told me in June of 1997, when I graduated, that by January of 1998 I'd have my own business I would have thought you were crazy. I started Community College of Philadelphia in September of 1997 – Community College because my S.A.T. scores were so low that my high school counselor told me, "Mike, with these scores, they won't even let you in the parking lot of one these universities here in Philly." I just was not a "standardized test" student. Later, I discovered that "standard" just wasn't good enough for me anyway!

I had taught martial arts and helped out around the martial arts school where I trained for a few years. Sometimes I earned money doing it and sometimes I didn't. I did it

5

because I just loved it so much. I also worked at a local supermarket part time as a grocery bagger. I actually "moved up" to grocery checker/cashier after I achieved "bagger of the year" in 1996. Audiences laugh when I tell them about my prestigious "bagger of the year" award.

So there I was three months out of high school, starting Community College and working as a part-time cashier. A week into my first semester of college I "withdrew." That's another way of saying that I dropped out, mainly because I signed up for all of the wrong classes for all of the wrong reasons. Later we'll talk about how important passion is in anything you pursue.

I was sitting in the back room of the supermarket on break. A guy who also worked there named Bruno was on break the same time I was. Bruno was what they called in the store, a "lifer." At the time he was in his late thirties and had been working there for close to fifteen years.

I'm originally from South Philly. When you think of a guy from South Philly named Bruno, you probably think of a guy with a big gold chain and chest hair showing through his halfway unbuttoned shirt. South Philly has a lot of "Mafia look-alikes." But that was not this South Philly Bruno! He looked like a scruffy

George Costanza (Jerry's best friend on Seinfeld).

At first glance the average person would dismiss Bruno. I mean come on, here is a guy who looks like a less well-kept version of George Costanza. Who lived with his mother and worked as a cashier in a supermarket. You'd be wrong though. Bruno was pretty smart. He was a college grad. His brothers were pretty prominent people, one a doctor, one a lawyer. His family owned some investment type real estate. Bruno's father passed away many years before and he sort of took on the role of "looking after mom."

He must have noticed that I seemed a little down as I sat there in the break room. Then he asked: "So Mike, how is school going?" I told him that I withdrew.

Then he said, "So, you dropped out, huh?" He then asked me what I planned to do. I told him, "I'm not sure, but I won't be working here forever." He started to probe a little. He said, "You do the martial arts stuff right?" I said, "Yeah." He said, "Well, why don't you do that? You have a marketable skill." Here I was, just seventeen, and I'm thinking, what the heck is a "marketable skill?" He said, "You paid to learn martial arts right?" "Yes," I said. Then he said the words that got me in motion and gave me the little kick in the pants I needed. He said, "If you paid to learn martial arts, why wouldn't other people now pay you to teach them?"

Three months later, January 5th, 1998, to be exact, I opened my first martial arts school! By the way, I also started Community College again, this time taking business classes. The fact is that you never know when someone – anyone – will say something that can change or shape your life. It is so important to keep your mind open as you read this book! The other takeaway in this story is that I didn't "ponder it" too long. I didn't go and ask the naysayers what they thought. I got in motion!

Feel free to add this quote to your list of favorites...

"Don't Let Grass Grow Under Your Feet" - Marcel, The Carpet Guy

It's funny how you get advice at awkward times or from someone you don't see as the type who should be dispensing it, and hence you dismiss it. When I was twenty-three, I bought my first rental property in a pretty good South Philadelphia neighborhood. The property needed new carpets throughout. I called a carpet guy and he took care of the work. When he called to tell me he was done I told him to come by my office and pick up a check. At the time, my office was in the business that I owned and operated. As I was handing him the check, he was asking me questions like how old I was and how long I've had my own business. He concluded the conversation by saying, "Mike, don't let grass grow under your feet." At that time, it simply went in one ear and out the other. Maybe my twenty-three year old ego said, "What's this carpet guy talking about?" Years later it dawned on me that he was right! We must stay in motion. Life has a strange way of sneaking up on you. But if you're in motion toward your most desired goals you'll be alert and able to deal with the inevitable sneak attack!

When you begin to get in motion, you will also be "acted upon" by outside forces. These outside forces come in the form of delays, miss-communications, missed opportunities and other events that are usually out of your control. When these forces act on you, just continue ahead and work hard to regain your pace.

Here's an example:

Carol Frank, author of Do As I Say, Not As I Did, tells stories of entrepreneurs who ran into extremely difficult circumstances. Carol tells her own story in her book. Carol had a successful birdcage business. Her primary manufacturer began selling her very same birdcage designs to a competitor with the aim of putting her out of business. In the end, she recovered and eventually sold her business for a hefty sum. Had she not continued her forward motion, her business would have gone bust. If she waited for some outside force or some "positive motivation" before finding a new supplier and getting her company back on track, her story may not have had such a happy ending.

Carol Frank shared many lessons from the school of hard-knocks with me in a special audio interview. You can get a copy of the entire interview by going to: www.askmiked.com/carol

---

Here's the point, and let's be honest here: it's tough to be motivated when adversity is staring you right in the face. It's tough to get motivated when life keeps throwing crap at you. Motivation is only possible when you get going and get on with it.

Newton's Second Law

Acceleration is produced when a force acts on a mass. The greater the mass (of the object being accelerated) the greater the amount of force needed (to accelerate the object).

Heavier objects require more force to move the same distance as lighter objects.

The more excess baggage you carry in the form of fear, worry and anger, the heavier you'll be and the more force you will require to get to where you want to be. Feel free to fact check this; Once I read how the part of the brain that's engaged when you are in a "state" of doing what you love, the prefrontal cortex, cannot operate when you are over-run by fear and worry. Those emotions come from a different part of the brain, the amygdala.

Both regions cannot operate at the same time. The object of the game is to not be forceful at all. The object of the game is to get to where you want to be as fast as possible without feeling you have to "force it." Don't believe me? Have you ever tried to force someone to do something? Short of the "gun to the head method," force just doesn't work. Winning through the use of force ultimately boils down to who has more strength. I guess the use of force worked for Saddam Hussein for a while and it temporarily worked for Adolf Hitler, but in the end what happened? Sure you could argue that the United States uses force to protect certain principles and Countries around the world. But that's simply a matter of using necessary force to fight murderous forces radical in ideology! So let's get off the geo-political talk and get back to you...

What excess baggage is making you heavier? What is holding you back and therefore requiring you to use more "force" to get to where you want to be?

Is home life not going the way it should?

Are you not getting cooperation from others?

Is it you?

I learned from the great Brian Tracy that one of the best questions to ask yourself is: "What is it in me, that is holding me back?" Be honest!

Here's the good news...

Since the law states that acceleration takes place when a force acts on a mass, the more cooperation you get from other people and the more they buy into your vision, the faster you will accelerate toward your goals.

The very best way to get the cooperation from others that could lead to your acceleration is to be of service. Right now, there are people in your business, your community, your industry and your life that can accelerate your path to success. The first step is to identify who those people are and then do your best to be of service to them. The good news is usually this is real simple. The key, though, is to be extremely genuine.

When I began getting into motion toward my goal of being a respected leader in the industry that I worked everyone (big or small) who was already servicing my industry. I didn't expect much in return at all. Most of these people were very impressed by what I was able to contribute to their organizations.

It is imperative to your success that you reach out to those who can help you by first figuring out how you can help them. If you are in business locally, you can do that by joining a networking group. The best one I've come across is BNI. Just type "Business Network International" and then your state's name into a search engine and you'll find a list of local chapters. You can also find other local clubs and causes to contribute to like your Chamber of Commerce. Just be careful not to stretch yourself too thin.

Most of the people who work hard to get somewhere are constantly approached by people looking to leverage their influence and contacts. It's okay! They don't resent you at all for contacting them. But what they do look for is someone who stands out as different from everyone else who has an agenda. This is really true in the world of media. If you can stand out and offer something of value the media can be your golden ticket. Of course, everyone's goals are different.

The point is this:

Identify who can accelerate your success, and then figure out how you can serve them with no expectation of any immediate return. Then, if you do get an immediate return you'll be that much further ahead of the game.

You can only "move" toward your goals. "Pushing" will not work because of ... Newton's Third Law

For every action, there is an equal and opposite reaction.

For every force there is a reaction force that is equal in size, but opposite in direction. That is to say that whenever an object pushes another object, it gets pushed back in the opposite direction equally hard.

One night, when Julia and Marissa were still small, Jamie and I were doing our normal post-bath tag team routine to get the little sweeties ready for bed. Out of nowhere, Marissa, the younger one, charged at Julia and pushed her right up against the wall. Before

I could say, "Marissa, what are you crazy?" Julia bounced off the wall and pushed her back into the sink!

Have you ever felt like the problems of your life are constantly pushing you up against a wall? The natural thing to do is push back. But pushing back may only make things worse! The key is to see every problem as an opportunity to get in motion toward your goals. At times pushing back might be a good idea, but other times side-stepping the push or getting out of there can serve you well.

For a while I wrote a column for one of the trade publications in my industry. When you do what I do for a living - writing, speaking, consulting, and simply helping people - generally, it is wise to embrace, leverage and appreciate the opportunity to contribute to various publications. I frequently get interviewed by people who run audio and printed publications small, large and all-sizes-in-between. I am very liberal with my work being published as long as I am given credit and my Web Sites (www.AskMikeD.com or CyberspacetoYourPlace.com) and contact info is in the resource box. When a small or medium-sized business hires me and my company as consultants, to design them a website or to do copy-writing for their brochures and sales letters, it is usually because they were exposed to me somewhere. In my line of work (helping people and companies achieve greater success), it's the content that is powerful.

People read the content in my books, my articles and blog posts, they hear me speak somewhere and then they make the decision to come to me. That's just the nature of the beast! I don't tell people that I can help them - they decide if I can and then contact me. You can see why having a steady column in the trade publication of the industry I served was important to me. But when the publication changed owners, the new owners decided to "can" my column. Basically we just did not see eye to eye. At first, this seemed like a real problem. But when you quickly get into motion, a problem becomes an opportunity for growth – two months after the column disappeared, I started working with more organizations than I did for the entire two years my column was published. In short, after getting the column "canned" I got in motion and forged more productive relationships.

I could have pushed back and tried to get my column to stay in the magazine. But why fight a losing battle where the odds are against you? I never talked negatively about the man who canned my column other than to say that we just don't see eye to eye. In fact, I achieved more recognition in my industry without the column than with it!

When you see problems as opportunities to get in motion on a new path to reach your goals as opposed to trying to push back, you end up with the motivation to keep going in the face of adversity. If you let problems derail you, you end up getting stuck in human inertia.

Chapter 3

Motion And Motivation

"We cannot do everything at once, but we can do something at once" (Calvin Coolidge)

Motion: An act, process or instance of moving.

The keyword in the definition of motion is "act!" As human beings, we have the choice to act or be acted upon. We have the choice to be pro-active and do things out of purpose, passion and goals. Or, we can be re-active and do things based on knee-jerk impulses with little or no thought, purpose or goals. What will bring you closer to your most desired outcomes on a daily basis is pro-active motion. Of course some reactions need to come fast, like slamming on the brakes if you see the car in front of you slam on its brakes. But let's explore pro-active motion...

Pro-active Motion

Pro-active motion is the motion you take based on solid principles, information and passion. Pro-active motion will enable you to think two, three or even four moves ahead. Pro-active motion will help you remain calm, control your stress levels and easily deal with the curve balls and setbacks of daily life. Pro-active motion is planned.

Of course, each day is going to bring forth something that demands your attention immediately. I always plan my day and realistic objectives around the inevitable interruptions that come up. Some interruptions are totally welcomed and some are not. If a customer calls you to order more of your product, that is a welcomed interruption. The key to good customer service is to be sure the customer never gets the feeling that they are interrupting or bothering you. I once got a letter from the state telling me I was about to be fined $112,000.00. As you can imagine, that was an UN-welcomed interruption.

Pragmatism and appreciation have formed my principles and rules when it comes to customer service. I frequently get questions from my clients via email and if I am able to, I answer them quickly and in detail. I value feedback and the opinions of anyone who is subscribing to a program of mine. I once got an email from a user of a new product. The subject of the email read PROBLEM WITH PRODUCT. In my younger years, I might have "re-actively" dealt with the situation the wrong way. After all, she was the only one reporting "problems."

But this customer actually had some very good observations that were right on target. I addressed the issues and encouraged her to feel free to contact me with any other suggestions.

The beauty of pro-active motion lies in the fact that you will always get to choose your reactions. Choosing the proper reactions and responses are key. I once interviewed Hal Runkel for an audio magazine I published called *Raising Real Winners*. Hal is the author of *Scream Free Parenting*. He's been on NBC's The Today Show and many other programs. What he told me about *Scream Free Parenting* truly applies to life. With *Scream Free Parenting*, the strategy is to exercise control over the only person you can control, and that is you! Believe me, it works, because you can't "control" your kids! Hal's advice applies to all of life, not just parenting.

> **Reminder: Go to my website, AskMikeD.com from some free stuff.**

What I call "pro-active motions" are simply actions based on helping you reach your goals.

A Productivity (And Sanity) Tip

As you make out your daily to-do list, be sure it is based on your short term and long term goals. Then, shorten it by one or two items per day. This way if you do get sidetracked, you won't end the day feeling as though you didn't get to most of your list. One of the keys to staying in positive motion and living the life you want is to use the power of momentum in your favor. If you are setting yourself up for failure by creating a "to-do" list that is too long and inflexible, you will only slow your momentum. I am not asking you to be less ambitious, just flexible.

Pro-Actively Plan Your Re-Active Motions

I know the above sentence may look like verbal Jiu-Jitsu. What it means is that you must remember that part of your everyday life will be filled with situations in which you'll have to react quickly. More people have been "tripped up" in the blink of an eye because of improper reactions. The key is to plan your reactions in advance. I know this may seem difficult. The secret is to have goals that have been programmed into your subconscious mind. We'll talk about this later.

Here's a great example:

I've been involved in martial arts since I was thirteen years old. When you learn self-defense through martial arts training, it is totally fake. But the synthetic experience, when practiced, can prepare you for a real-life situation. I have also had some self-defense training that was based on "adrenal stress response." This self-defense training comes as close to real life as possible. The program was developed by a gentleman by the name of Paten Quinn. Mr. Quinn discovered that even highly trained martial artists could not effectively use their skills in a real and life-threatening situation.

He noticed that even if they were able to call on some of their years of training, the movements and techniques did not come close to how well they were executed in the gym without the stress of a real situation. Adrenaline, when not controlled and used properly, made their years of training worthless. Mr. Quinn had his students train with heavily padded instructors who would play the role of assailants. They would use swear words and fight dirty just like a real-world criminal would. The result of using this type of training on his self-defense students was amazing. They were able to effectively defend themselves under the stress of a real situation because that is how they trained. It's really about controlling impulses and stress in tough situations, while still responding quickly and effectively. Easier said than done, yes! Let me give you another example from the world of parenting...

Louise Latham is the wife of the late Dr. Glenn

Latham who wrote a book called *The Power of Positive Parenting*. Louise told me a story of a parent who had success with one of the principles in the book. The principle is to plan out "reactions" in advance (Pro-active Reactions). A woman was consistently having negative behavioral issues with her adopted teenaged daughter. A feeling of tension came over her as she was getting ready go in to the living room to remind her daughter to do the vacuuming in the house. Of course, the daughter protested and told her mother she would not be vacuuming and her mother could do it herself.

At this point most parents would fly off the handle and "react" with something like, "Now you listen to me young lady!" But this positive parent carefully planned out her reaction. In a calm voice she informed her daughter that she understands that she does not want to do it, but will indeed have to as part of her household responsibilities. She did not get angry or upset. She did not "push" back or use force because in this type of situation it would not have worked. Later, the daughter picked up the vacuum without even being reminded and took care of her responsibility. Afterward, she hugged her mother and told her how sorry she was for acting the way she did. Basically, this successful parent knew in advance how she was going to react to the stress of the situation. She then executed control over the only person she has control over and consequently avoided a fight while strengthening the relationship.

Motivation: To Provide With A Motive

The word motive is directly related to action and motion. We have already discussed that getting in motion will generate more motivation. Motivation cannot come first because the simple act of starting requires and delineates that you are now in motion. So how do you get from standing still or moving away from your goals to getting in motion and moving toward your goals quickly? The answer is found in a six-letter word: Desire.

Desire is the starting point of all achievement. It is the "Why" of success. If I am driving down a road in my town that it is filled with pot holes and come across a man (or woman) performing road work with a jack-hammer, I know why he is doing the work – because the winters up here in New Hampshire take a toll on the asphalt and this road now needs fixing. And once you establish a why, you can then go on to the hows and the whats.

Your "why" must come first though! With a strong enough "why," the "hows" will come and so will the "whats". Why fix the road? To make it safer. How? I really don't know but the worker does. What does he do to fix the road? Again, I write and speak and consult and don't do roadwork, but I trust the guy knows what to do.

Five Simple Steps...

1) The desire - why you want to accomplish something
2) Setting yourself in motion toward the goal
3) The how and what you are going to do each day to achieve the goal
4) The motivation to keep going! (comes about because you are in motion)
5) Learn from your experiences and keep moving

Colonel Sanders is famous for his fried chicken recipe that eventually became the staple of KFC. He had been selling chicken to passers-by for many years. Then, the town he was in completed construction of a
new highway. The new highway took people right by his location without giving them an option to even see his little restaurant. His restaurant was soon out of business. As an aging man, he decided to get into motion. Why? Perhaps the desire not to let his chicken recipe and methods die on the vine. Or not to have something out of his control dictate the

way he would spend the rest of his life. He began to sell his "system" and the rest is history.

Let your "why" get you into motion and the motivation to figure out the how's and the what's will be there!

Chapter 4

How to Get More Done and Have More Fun Everyday

"We are what we repeatedly do. Excellence then, is not an act, but a habit" (Aristotle)

We all have the same twenty-four hours in a day.

Let's reveal five simple strategies to help you achieve more with the twenty-four hours you get every day. It's a gift right? That's why they call it the "present?" Not a bad way to look at it. Here are some ways to get more out of every day.

Get up earlier - I frequently study happy and successful businesspeople. One thing they all have in common is the habit of getting up early and getting going. You can accomplish this by getting to bed earlier or just conditioning yourself to require less sleep. I can function OK on between six and seven hours of sleep. I know there's always a new study about how sleeping more can prolong your life or sleeping less can prolong your life. Frankly, all the studies on sleep just confuse me! Figure out what works for you!

Exercise daily - Someone once told me to make it a rule to only exercise on the days you eat! When you exercise you'll give yourself more energy and you'll actually cause yourself to get a deeper night's sleep. For best results, exercise first thing in the morning and take "active breaks" throughout the day. But no more excuses; taking care of yourself is really important. Combine activities when possible. In the spring, summer and fall I encourage my girls to come "explore" the neighborhood with me. This way, we're spending time together and getting our exercise.

Take control of your schedule - Regain control of your time by minimizing distractions. Adopt a "closed door" policy for certain hours of the day. Doing so will help you get more out of each day. The time it takes to start and stop a project can add minutes and sometimes hours to the time it would normally take to complete it. If you work for someone who expects you to be "on call," be sure to discuss this with him or her. Explain the benefits of your new M.O.

Have everything ready to go - Imagine the surgeon saying "scalpel" and the nurse starts searching all over for it. Meanwhile the poor huckleberry is knocked out and waiting on the operating table! Fumbling for your "tools" throughout the day simply sucks your day dry of valuable time and energy you could be using to get more out of it. Have everything ready to go before you begin a task! I'm not afraid to admit that I have been guilty of this one on many occasions. I'm workin' on it though!

Get the most from every human interaction - Napoleon Hill, author of Think and Grow Rich, identified a "pleasing personality" as one of the key ingredients for success. Every human interaction you have during the course of the day will help you get a step closer to your goals or a step away from them. Remember to be calm and cool in every interaction with customers and colleagues. After you answer a question or fulfill a request, always ask your customers or colleagues, "Is that all you need?" or "Is there anything else I can do for you?" You will set yourself so far apart that you'll get ahead fast, become more influential and get more out of each day! I know this one in particular is not easy because there are so many flaky and just plain wacky people around. But as you continue to move forward and forge productive relationships with people who are "on the same page," many of the flakes and wackos will be less likely to bother you.

Using these five simple secrets will help you accomplish more in less time. Why not start applying them today?

***

Evergreen Success Principle

If It Is To Be, It's Up To Me

No one is coming to the rescue. Sure, people may choose (for themselves) to help you along the way. If you do get help, great! You got help because you inspired someone to help you or the person who helped you acted out of his own interest.

Take control of situations and be totally accountable for your results. Get things done, make things happen – it's up to you!

***

Chapter 5

Why <u>You</u> Are Your Most Valuable Asset

*"Do what you can, with what you have,
where you are" (T. Roosevelt)*

Most folks, ninety to ninety-five percent of them, will categorize their assets something like this - real estate, cars, cash, stocks, bonds or precious medals. They're not wrong! Some of them may possess a whole lot of these assets. But it would be foolish to think that any of these should be thought of as their most valuable asset.

If you haven't been tempted to use your house as an ATM machine and you've been paying down your mortgage, then you may have a balance sheet that looks something like this: Mortgage owed, $121,546.98; appraised value, $434,000.00. Therefore you'd have $312,453.02 of equity in your home, causing your net worth to go to the plus side by the same amount. Then, add in everything else minus any other debts and you end up with your total assets.

While the above two paragraphs are basic for

most of you reading this, I needed the example to point out how boring and really unimportant (in the grand scheme of things) the "traditional way" of figuring out your assets really is!

The reality is that YOU are your most valuable asset! And second place to you is that all-important commodity that we all possess, but will never know when we'll run out of: time! So let's start with calculating your value...

Everything that you have in your life (or don't have) is because of you. Your wife, your husband, your kids, your job, your business, your body, everything! I know your body is based on genetics and you inherited your spouse. Stay with me though...

Just as you subtract what you own from what you owe to find out your asset base, we can come up with a simple formula to figure out your personal assets. First, let's take your strengths. What are you good at? What do you bring to the table? What can you do better than the next guy? If it were real estate we were appraising, we'd figure this as "location, location, location." Next, what is your knowledge flow? What kind of quality information do you take in on a regular basis? Do you read good books on the subjects of business and self-help? If this were a business, this would be the "cash flow." Yes, information and knowledge is THAT important. Now, this one is a tough one: How much time is left? Since you really never know you need to just factor in the average. Male life expectancy is about mid 70's on average - women can add eight more years to their life expectancy. This would be like "depreciation."

The above formula is definitely not a mathematical certainty. (I challenge one of you arithmetically gifted readers to come up with that and then get in touch with me). But don't miss the value in thinking of your life in this context. Your strengths are what you have going for you. However, there are certain things that decrease your asset value.

For instance, if you're older, you have, hopefully, more priceless wisdom stored up but less time to personally use it. Sorry, that's just the way it is. I do believe that it will benefit you in the next life! More importantly than how much time you have left, keep an eye on the items you can control that will destroy your value...

How's your health? Are you taking care of your physical body? If not, it's going to devalue YOU! Are you being careful of the messages you allow into your mind? Since all messages are stored by the subconscious mind they are either an asset or a liability. How's your thought process? Is it positive and optimistic overall, or filled with fear and doubts?

The important concept to keep in mind is that YOU are your most valuable asset! Therefore, you need to be constantly improving, learning, and growing!

Give yourself a fair appraisal. Next, take steps to boost your asset value. Just remember a couple key areas that make the most difference in boosting your value: Take care of yourself mentally by getting on a good mental diet, and take care of yourself physically by staying active!

Always remember that the choice of going forward is all up to you. You're worth far more than anything that shows up on your financial balance sheet! So get moving!

Chapter 6

How to Overcome Your Limitations

"There are no limitations to the mind except those we acknowledge" (Napoleon Hill)

If you are a fan of success literature, you will no doubt have heard the saying that all limitations are self-imposed.

But, are all limitations "self-limitations?"

If all limitations are self-imposed, what about the speed limit? Someone's telling you how fast you can drive, right? Imagine if you had to drive 100 miles to your destination and you had one hour to get there. Then, imagine if you don't get there in an hour you are going to drop dead! That speed limit of sixty-five mph is not really working for you now is it? Others have imposed their limitations on you!

Some people impose limitations on you because they are trying to protect you. What are they trying to protect you from? Failure really! They don't want you to suffer the consequences of things not working out. The truth is your life will play out according to the choices you make. And the sooner things start to play out, the sooner you can correct your course if need be.

Getting into that bad business relationship I told you about was painful. It's tempting to wish that it never happened. But if it had never happened, would I have ever sat down and written these words? Would you be reading these words? The initial decision of entering the relationship that went sour led to the motion of getting out, then ultimately, to greater success. That led to the motivation and wisdom (still a lot to learn) to pursue new and exciting goals. You can do the same. Sure, my lawyer and a few people close to me were trying to protect me by saying, "Are you sure you want to do this?" And they all had my best interest at heart. But I moved forward anyway. Ultimately, it was a lesson I needed to learn on my own. Even though they were trying to help, others were attempting to impose limitations on me.

Why Else Will They Put Limitations On You?

Some do it because they just don't want you to succeed! If you succeed they think it means less for them. The scarcity mentality infects a lot of people. When these folks offer you their well-meaning advice (limitations), thank them and move on.

What About Self-Imposed Limitations?

They are the product of a couple of things. Your upbringing can play a major role in the limitations you place on yourself later in life. Of course if you were told things like, "You are no good," it will take its toll, but it can be beaten. Joe Girard, the only salesman to make it into the *Guinness Book of World Records*, tells the story of how his father constantly told him he'd end up a criminal and a loser. For many years, Joe battled that voice which, unfortunately, proved his father right on many occasions. But when Joe made it big and was speaking at the same seminar as former President Ford, he looked up into the heavens at his father and said, "Dad, you were wrong!"

We all have had some negative programming. The best way to override the negative programming is to get some positive momentum by taking action. Begin to set small goals and then put in motion the activities and behavior needed to accomplish them. As you do, your motivation will increase and your limitations will decrease. Success feeds success. Inch by inch, it's a cinch!

***

Evergreen Success Principle

We Become What We Think About Most Of The Time!

Focus on and think about what you want and how you are going to get it! It is easy to dwell on problems and obstacles. That's what most people do.

Discipline yourself to take control over the only thing you do have control over - your very own thoughts! The great Earl Nightingale taught this so well, in his famous "The Strangest Secret."

***

Chapter 7

It's Like Having A "Smelly Cat" In The House

"Now is the time. Needs are great, but your possibilities are greater" (Bill Blackman)

I know not every cat owner has the smell of cats in their house. But you certainly know the smell I am talking about! It's the one that blasts you in the face when you walk into a house that has it. The funny thing is this: if you happen to find yourself in a house infested with the odor and you asked the homeowner if she plans on doing anything about it she'd almost always say, "What smell are you talking about? I don't smell anything!" She has simply become immune to it from being around it so long. It's like it doesn't exist.

When I owned my martial arts school in Philadelphia we'd occasionally get the out-spoken mom who would say in a very loud voice, "Man it stinks in here like sweat and feet – are you guys gonna do anything about it?" We did our best considering there were over 200 kids, parents and hardcore training adults coming in and out of our little studio.

43

But the truth was "fresh smelling" to us was stinky to the normal nose!

So it is with being stuck in a rut, stuck in a bad relationship, stuck in business or a job that is not going anywhere. Sometimes others can see you are stuck, but you are too close to see the obvious and you have also become somewhat immune to change. When I work with clients in my business consulting practice, it is easy for me to see what they cannot. An extra set of eyes (or an extra nose) can be so valuable.

Don't hear or read anything I'm not saying...

What I am not saying is to just listen to anyone who thinks they know what is in your best interest. Let me give you a personal example. What if someone says to you that the person you have chosen as a mate is a loser and that you should dump him and get on with it? Well, if you happen to love the person they are referring to with all of your heart and that person, despite their shortcomings, makes you happy, then you should run in the opposite direction as quickly as possible.

When my wife and I moved to New Hampshire, she started a new job and I started a new business. (Talk about change, motion and motivation!) Anyway, for about two months into our new lives, my wife's mother lived with us. She had been living with us for about a year already before we made the move. Jamie and I invited her to live with us after the passing of Jamie's father.

Times were tough! We were coming out of that horrible business relationship that nearly bankrupted us and starting a new business, and Jamie was starting a new job. Despite that, we still gave her mother money each week for watching our girls. The problem was that we were funding her wine drinking and her petty gambling habits. I don't know if you have ever lived with someone who has an addiction (minor or major), but it is not easy. I was able to recognize all of the warning signs because I witnessed my brother's addiction to drugs for almost five years. I saw what it did to my mother and father.

Jamie's mother slowly started to unravel. Starting a few weeks after the move, when Jamie would come home from work after a long day she would complain about how I would just sit in my office and "play on my computer" or "talk on the phone" while she (Jamie) was out "working." There was really no point in trying to explain that I was building a new business and doing my own telephone sales. As far as I was concerned, I did not have to explain anything about how many people now work from home! The funny thing was just a few years before when the money was flowing, I could do no wrong in my mother-in-law's eyes. Criminal investigators "follow the money." The principle works in life too when you are trying to figure out why someone is causing you grief!

Finally, we were able to see so clearly that Jamie's mother's intention was to see Jamie and I in divorce court. Later we actually found some weird "curse-like" writings designed to split up marriages. I kid you not!

She was determined to manipulate Jamie in order to "get rid of me." The resentment toward me probably started years back when we lent her almost $30,000, so that she and Jamie's father would not lose their home to foreclosure. We demanded that when the house was sold, we get it all back plus other debts that were owed to us. Jamie finally had it with the negativity and called one of her brothers from New Jersey to come get her mother and bring her back there to live on her own.

Her mother was in fine health and quite capable of taking care of herself. She also qualified for temporary government assistance.

The icing on the cake came a few months later when we received a certified letter from the Ocean County Courthouse that we were being sued by my mother-in-law for "back pay." I guess for watching her grand-kids while she was living in our house, eating our food and enjoying our warm air in the winter and cold air in the summer. To avoid a default court judgment against us we had to drive twelve hours round trip to defend ourselves. The judge ruled in our favor.

The lesson? There are four.

One - Not everyone who offers you the "Can you smell that cat advice?" has your best interest in mind. Jamie's mother was trying to give her (Jamie) some invalid "smelly cat advice." Best to be like my wife and get to the crux of the issue, then move forward accordingly. Ultimately it was Jamie and I who had to get rid of the "smelly cat."

Two - Don't let anyone... mother, sister, brother or children rob you of your precious time on this planet.

Three - People can only help themselves (which we'll learn more about later). Sometimes, when you take drastic action to ensure your own happiness by getting rid of smelly cats, you help enable the other person to change.

Four - The world is abundant! Shortly after my mother-in-law embarrassed herself in civil court trying to sue her daughter and me, she got on her feet, got a job and became independent.

For Jamie and me, the motivation to find qualified child care and adjust our lives according to not having someone around who can watch the kids between certain hours came after we put in motion the removal of my mother-in-law from our everyday lives.

I know when I share this story about us "kicking" my mother-in-law out of our house; it is at the risk of getting hate mail. "How could you? How could Jamie do that to her mother?" Jamie and I knew right away we made the right choice. Your gut will tell you when it is time to take the "cat in the house advice" or get the person out of your life who is giving you the wrong "cat in the house advice." Your nose will you tell when to get the "smelly cat" out of the house.

The funny thing is that for years, people asked us how we put up with her. I guess they "smelled the cat," but we couldn't.

So what is stinking up your life? What is it that

is so obvious to those around you who really do care about you without an agenda of their own? Is it a relationship? Is it a job? And be honest with yourself. If you've got the "smelly cat" odor, do something about it! Only you know what change you need to put in motion.

***

Evergreen Success Principle

Don't Become A S.N.I.O.P. "Susceptible to the Negative Influences of Other People"

I originally learned "SNIOP" from the great Zig Ziglar. If you allow yourself to be affected by the negativity of others, you will qualify as a SNIOP. Being a SNIOP can kill your forward motion toward your goals.

The big question to ask yourself: Am I going to allow others to take me off course and sabotage my success?

***

Chapter 8

Attention Is Reward

"My life is one long obstacle course, with me being the chief obstacle" (Jack Paar)

Sorrow, mistakes, sickness, rut jobs and problems are a part of life. But the more attention you give them, the more you encourage them to settle in. Before you know it, the years have passed! Every successful person, defined as someone living life on their own terms while bringing value and joy to others, has indeed gone through some tough times. Even when times are tough you must focus your attention on taking the kind of action that will ultimately lead to your victory.

Attention is a kind of reward. Pay attention to the experiences that pay off the most. Stop dwelling on your mistakes and start concentrating on studying your achievements and successes, however small they may be.

Study your mistakes ever so briefly and just extract the lessons and take the wisdom with you. People who make the same mistakes over and over again are lacking in common sense. Don't reward your past failures by reliving them in your mind; they don't deserve your attention. As an NFL quarterback needs a short memory, so do you when it comes to mistakes!

Suppose you have failed at something, or not done well at it - won't other people hold that against you? They probably will temporarily; that's reality. But there are ways to overcome it. One simple way is to allow your actions to begin speaking for you. If others see you improving, then your actions are building your credibility. It's the motion to improve that counts. You'll win over the trust of others and gain momentum for future success.

"If you can't make good at one thing," says tradition, "how can you expect to make good at something else, something bigger?" But let's say you are a good quarterback, and the coach puts you in at tackle. You play your heart out and get slaughtered. That still doesn't mean you're not a good quarterback. You might have won the game playing in your rightful position. Put yourself and others in "positions" where each of you will shine. There's no need to spend your life doing something or giving attention to activities that don't get you results! And chances are if you're not good at something, your results will reflect it.

Notice here I don't talk about just doing what you love or what you enjoy only. That is not pragmatic, especially as you are starting off. You may possess a valuable skill that you must exploit to earn your keep; whether you still take great joy in it all the time doesn't matter! Sometimes you need to "just do it" as you are working toward something else that you find more rewarding. The truth is I really don't always enjoy picking up the phone and following up on leads for my business. But you know what, the many years as a business owner have taught me that when I hustle a little, it pays off. Once I get going on it, I actually don't mind it either. See, motion before motivation. Doing what you know you need to do to move you forward helps you give attention to your goals.

The fine line...

If we ever find ourselves in a position of rewarding attention to something that we no longer enjoy, then we must take practical, logical, rational and non-emotional steps to begin doing something we do enjoy that will help us reach our life and financial goals. It may make sense for you to just "jump in" or it may not. You be the judge! You can start something new in just a few minutes every day. As long as you discipline yourself and keep your commitment to you, eventually you will make the transition 100% to your new life. Now here's the kicker...

Your ideal life starts when you decide it does. That's the "Success Secret That Never Fails," because you are taking action on reaching goals that are important to you. Then, even if you do mess up, you take the wisdom with you and get stronger. Just be sure to give attention to your little successes along the way.

It's also common to look for what's wrong with people, rather than for what's right about them. The problem with giving attention to what is wrong with other people is you'll end up getting more of what's wrong. Of course, there are times when you need to draw the line and get someone out of your personal, business or career life. Just keep in mind to give attention to the good things when it comes to people who are closest to you. Your spouse, your kids, your parents, maybe your in-laws and those close business associates you have interdependent relationships with. Reward the good stuff with positive attention. Pay attention to what needs to be improved and then get in motion to improve, don't dwell on it.

Chapter 9

The Uncomplicated Cure
For Procrastination

*"For every action, there is an equal or opposite
criticism" (Author unknown)*

I am not some expert on how to beat
procrastination. But I have learned through my
own experience and by paying attention to
other people that some actually procrastinate
via perfectionism.

I sometimes wonder if perfectionism and
procrastination are closely related. By
definition these two words are worlds apart.
But the truth is, going for perfection in
everything feeds procrastination. And
procrastination has killed more hopes and
dreams than any other human tendency.

We all procrastinate – it's natural to put things
off. The danger is in putting things off until
"the time is just right." When that happens you
end up dressing "the wolf" of procrastination
in the "sheep's clothing" of perfectionism.

At first glance striving for perfection seems like

a good idea. In a competitive business environment, being "perfect" may give you an edge over your competition. But if your competition is busy servicing clients and customers while you're still tying up all of your loose ends, then it really doesn't matter how perfect you are. Of course when it comes to gas pedals that could get stuck or oil wells that could leak perfection is a good idea!

In life, it is important to always "better your best." In business, striving to do things better than your competition is a must. Striving for perfection is something that you'll always work for but never achieve. But the good news is, you must stay in motion as you are striving. Therefore, it is impossible for you to "wait" until things are perfect before you set out. If you are working as you are striving then you are OK. If you are waiting and waiting and waiting, then that is no good and you will hold yourself back. Let me give you an example.

After the first version of this book was published and it became a bestseller on Amazon.com I actually went back into the manuscript and fixed a couple of things. Good authors are always learning and testing new ideas in their lives, and I am no different. Plus, the more I write the better I get. So the truth is this version is a little better than the first. It's not perfect, but just a little better. If I had decided to wait for the "perfect" manuscript, well, I'd still be waiting and you wouldn't be reading!

Striving (key word) for perfection requires you to get in motion. "Waiting" for things to be perfect is procrastination by default. Procrastination is the opposite of getting in motion. So get it done and get it out there and you can "strive" for perfection as you are also making things happen.

Most people will procrastinate and justify their procrastination as a quest for perfection. Make no mistake about it – taking action and getting in motion give you the real edge over the competition.

Nothing is perfect and nothing ever will be. Everything that you and I produce will have some sort of human error wrapped somewhere in it. Of course, the above fact doesn't give you permission to produce shabby work either. What it does do is liberate you from procrastination via perfectionism. And just like the quote that started this chapter tells us, it doesn't matter how perfect your work is - it is still going to be criticized by someone. Combine your obsession with perfection with a bias for getting in motion and you can't lose!

Chapter 10

The Chicken Nugget Theory Of Success

*"Experience is not what happens to a man;
it is what a man does with what happens
to him" (Aldous Huxley)*

I remember watching the movie "Super Size Me" about the gentleman who went on a total McDonald's diet for a full month. In one particular part of the movie, they were showing how Chicken McNuggets were made. They are basically made from parts of many different chickens. The process was certainly not healthy or appetizing, but it made me formulate the "Chicken Nugget Theory of Success." It goes like this...

Our lives are sort of like chicken nuggets in a sense. Think about it; we take bits and pieces of wisdom, knowledge and unique experiences and create our own set of skills, strategies, and viewpoints. Some of these pieces are good, while some can be hurtful.

If you read twenty to thirty minutes per day and you read at an average rate, you may knock down one or so books per week. The kind of books I'm referring to are non-fiction. I don't have anything against fiction; I just have yet to ever make the time to get into fiction books. Most books I read are informational or inspirational in nature, like this one. If you read twenty to thirty minutes per day on any given topic you will become an expert in that topic within a few years. How will you become an expert? Because most people don't read anything at all! By reading you are giving yourself a huge advantage over the next guy and putting some healthy pieces into your nugget.

Listening to and taking in positive messages can be helpful too. There are so many "audio of the month" type programs and most good books can also be purchased in audio form. You can turn your driving time into productive learning time. You can also listen to quality information while you perform simple tasks like exercising, emptying the dishwasher or preparing meals. Get yourself a small MP3 player and put it to use. Of course, listen when it doesn't cause you to be rude to anyone or distract you from the task at hand.

I have some quality mp3 recordings on my website: www.askmiked.com. While you're there be sure to sign up for my e-newsletter and updates.

What's Not So Healthy to Your Nuggets?

Too much negativity! If you're not careful these ingredients can quickly override your positive input. Imagine you just completed a great course or book and you've got one more idea that adds to your puzzle. Maybe it builds on something you've learned elsewhere. You get the "Aha moment" and right away get into motion. Then, "bam!" You flip open the newspaper to read that the Dow Jones Industrial Average just dropped 700 points in one day. Out of curiosity you turn on the television and you're hit again with more negative news about the economy and a mass murder. Your inspiration is down and you're now thinking in "Oh No" mode!

Consciously, we know that we should plow forward toward our goals and ignore the negativity that is not directly affecting us. After all, that is the essence of "Motion Before Motivation." The problem is that just like those nuggets get their parts from all of those different chickens, your subconscious mind records all of the information you allow to get through to it. Once that information is recorded, it is part of you forever. And you know what goes in must come out in some way.

I'm not like some authors and speakers who tell you to "turn off the news." No way! You need to stay informed. Just know when enough is enough. We'll talk about the subconscious mind a little later. Until then, just let the news only get as far as your conscious mind by not allowing yourself to take in the same negative story over and over again.

Or Just Don't Participate In The Negativity...

I was once conducting a telephone seminar for some of my clients. The topic was "How to Grow Your Business Even in a Recession." One of the guest speakers told us about a situation where a customer asked him if he felt as though he should be dropping his prices for her because of the "recession." He politely said, "Ma'am, have you lost your job? Are you having trouble paying your bills?" She responded, "No, I am doing just fine." He said: "So am I. Aren't *we* fortunate that *we* are not in a recession?" She agreed and then proceeded with the purchase. Her thoughts were being affected by the negativity that was being dumped into her mind by the people around her.

Controlling what goes into your mind, and doing your best to allow only the "good stuff" in will help you utilize the power of your mind more effectively. Motion Before Motivation is built on pressing forward regardless. However, you are only human. So why not stack the odds in your favor by keeping your nuggets in check?

****

Evergreen Success Principle

The Movie Theatre In Your Mind

You can make your mind into a little movie theater. You can sit there and watch movies whereby you are the star. You can mentally picture what you want. It can be a goal that you have or the life you desire. The key is to see yourself living it as you are sitting there watching the movie.

To really make this concept work for you, discipline yourself for maybe five or ten minutes a day. You can be in the shower or you can just be hanging out - it does not matter. Just go into the theater of your mind and picture yourself successful.

***

Chapter 11

Spectator Vs Participant

"A quitter never wins and a winner never quits"
(Napoleon Hill)

I've heard Zig Ziglar, one of America's most sought after speakers for many years, say life is not a spectator sport. He is totally right! Yet we spend thousands of hours being spectators - watching, listening, and being entertained. That's why entertainment is big bucks, because we all constantly seek it. We all deserve to be entertained for sure. But think about being a spectator or an active participant in your own life. Remember, being an active participant means you are in motion!

We'll define it in two ways: If you're letting your life happen, you're being a spectator. If you're making your life happen, then you are a participant. If you're just passively looking at your results, you're being a "spectator." If you ask yourself, "What can I do to get better results?" then you are a participant.

Where you're at now, at this very moment, is a result of our past actions (participant) or inactions (spectator). However, you must remember that your current situation is truly not an accurate representation of who you currently are - it's who you were. Don't get the wrong idea though; your behaviors are you and they will shape the future you.

To make the *Spectator VS Participant* idea work for you just focus more on being a participant. If you actively get into motion with the behaviors that will make you who you want to be then you will create the life you want! The key is to stop observing your current realities and to begin creating the realities you want based on getting into motion and participating in the kind of behaviors that will lead you to your goals.

Before I was published as an author and before I began speaking as a second career, I made it a point to write for thirty to sixty minutes per day. When I was twenty-three years old, I joined Toastmasters so I could practice speaking to groups and get over any fears I had about speaking. I purchased training from some of the best in the speaking business before I was speaking regularly. I sent numerous ideas and articles to various publications. I was shot down many times, but I slowly started getting more and more out there.

It would have been easy for me to say, "I own a martial arts school, that's what I do. I'm not yet a speaker or writer, so why should I speak or write?" The lesson is that you must begin participating in the activities that you want to make up your ideal life. In most cases, you'll be "participating" in your new ideal life before it actually takes shape. Begin participating in the life you desire and you'll soon be living it. Remember, Motion Before Motivation. The time will never be just right, so be a participant!

***

Evergreen Success Principle

What You Put Into Your Mind Today Will Determine Where You End Up Tomorrow!

The information that goes into your mind will influence your thoughts. Your thoughts will influence your emotions. As we are all more emotional than logical, your emotions will then influence your behavior. Your behavior will influence your daily results. Your daily results will bring you one step closer to or one step away from your goals.

Your mind does not care whether what you put into it is positive or negative. The equation will remain the same every time.

***

Chapter 12

So What Do You Really Want? Here's How to Find Out

*"Man is not the creature of circumstances.
Circumstances are the creatures of men"
(Benjamin Disraeli)*

By now you've got the message that the key to getting what you want is to get in motion toward achieving it. Taking action leads to the positive feelings that feed your success. You realize it is okay if you are not "motivated" all the time. By nature all human beings are lazy. But taking the first small step can make reaching the big goal possible.

Sometimes it is hard to figure out what the first step is. Should I create the product or first thoroughly research the market? Should I go rent the office before I have my first client? Should I join the health club or begin eating better first?

Here's one way to get your answers

Let's take the example of starting a business. If your "research" is just a front for never really doing any selling of your idea, product or concept, you are putting the wrong motion in action. Let's say that you have a product that solves a common household problem. Talk to people in your community and ask them if they are bothered by this problem and what they think could be done about it. Maybe you'll find out you have real value to offer others. The moment someone is willing to hand over their money to you because you solved a problem for them, you know you've got something! The shortest route to knowing whether you are putting the right motions into action (when it comes to launching some sort of business idea) is to see if you have created value for someone else.

Two personal examples of what NOT to do

In the beginning, I told you about the financially devastating venture I got involved in. No regrets here! But this will hopefully help you avoid doing something that will take a few years to undo. The problem in my case was that it was too early in the process to see how a particular industry would react to this type of business model. It did not react well! In all fairness and to communicate to you that I take personal responsibility for my mistake, I was not financially prepared to stay the course for the inevitable course corrections that are required early on in any venture as soon as the market gives you feedback.

The market provides feedback all the time. The dot com bubble was a great example. Young Internet entrepreneurs were buying jets and fancy offices with public money before they even sold a single product. The market gave feedback to residential real estate in the form of "boom and bust." And the market told GM and Chrysler that even though they sell as many cars as their Japanese counterparts, their business model was outdated and sucking them dry! With a little help their friends (the American tax payers) they turned things around.

My mother-in-law, who I told you about earlier, came up with a nifty little invention. It was not original at all but was certainly an improvement on the only other product we found in its category. Any parent knows when kids are first learning to walk, it can be a killer on the back! You've got to bend over and guide their every step. Her nice-looking device was classier than a leash and comfortable for the kid and the person guiding their steps. She named it "Just about Walking," because you use it for a baby that is, well, just about walking. I bought the domain name for my mother-in-law and handed her a book by Dan Kennedy called *How to Make Millions with Your*

Ideas. I figured, if she wants do this, the best way I can help her is to give her some good reading material to inform her. Jamie also told her to take Marissa, who was just about walking at the time, to a baby store so other parents could see the product in action. Unfortunately, she never got into motion or took any action to make the product a reality.

Here's the secret - "Just do it!"

If you want to get in shape and stay that way, make exercise and disciplined eating a part of your life. The problem is that most people will make a plan to get in shape for some impending event. Perhaps the summer's coming or they've been asked to be in a wedding. If they succeed in dropping the pounds or getting in shape, it ends up being only temporary. Jamie was a college athlete and was salsa dancing four nights per week when we first met. She was in great shape! And for a young shallow guy like me, she was it - beauty and brains! I often joke when I'm asked what my education level is that I write down "close to Ivy league grad." Most people can't help but do a double take and ask me what that means. I tell them that my wife graduated from Cornell, therefore I am "close to an Ivy League grad!" Anyway...

When Jamie was pregnant with Julia she put

on close to eighty pounds. Nineteen months later, Marissa was born. For a few years, Jamie's weight fluctuated and she was not happy about it. She would often say that she just was not "motivated" to exercise. A common problem of course! But one day she just made up her mind that she would join the health club near her office and work out four to five days a week. That decision has made her happier, healthier and "motivated" to keep it going! She now helps the whole family eat healthier and she teaches fitness classes a few nights per week. See what happens when you start!

If you are still unsure about taking the first step, it's OK. Some decisions have to be taken seriously and require you to move ahead with a little caution. But picture it sort of like a sliding scale. The more drastic the motion you take, the faster and with more force your feedback from the market (or from whatever else) will come. It is sad when you see the forensic shows about a woman in a long-term abusive relationship who finally musters up enough courage to leave only to send her so-called lover into a murderous rage – a drastic action that produced a drastic result! If she had taken action sooner, she may have not met the same fate. Think of my business debacle as a reminder that the more drastic the motion, the more drastic the feedback. This is neither good nor bad – it is just the way it is. One answer is to start easier with simple steps.

When you have solid goals it's easier to identify the first step to take.

Here's an exercise that can change your life and help you decide on which actions and which forward motion will be best for you.

I learned this from the great, Brian Tracy, and have modified it a little. Feel free to do the same.

Get a notebook and begin to write down your goals. A few mornings per week get into the habit of getting up fifteen minutes earlier than you currently do. If you don't allow for the extra time, you'll never get this done. Now here's the way it works...

Begin to write in your notebook your most desired goals. If you want to have $1,000,000 in the bank, write it down. If you want to be leader in your field, write it down. The key is to write it in the first person present tense. So you'd write, "I have $1,000,000 in the bank" or "I am a leader in my field." Thereafter, attach a date and year to each goal. Be realistic but ambitious.

On the bottom half of the page or simply after

you are done writing your goals, write down some of the qualities you'll need to possess to accomplish your goals. For example, if you want to be a recognized leader in your field, you'll most likely need to polish your public speaking skills. So you write down, "I am an excellent public speaker!"

Organized Day Dreaming

I read an article in *Psychology Today* about how new studies reveal that "day-dreaming" is good. The truth is that many successful people have known this for a long time! As you write down your goals you can also imagine them and see them in your mind. Your imagination can reveal to you breakthroughs, help you solve your current problems and help you rehearse for important real-life situations. The same article also mentioned that children who watch an average of three hours or more of TV per day are less imaginative than children who watch only one hour per day. So cut down on the TV time and spend a little more time in your own mind thinking about your most desired goals! Your imagination is like a muscle, and the more you work it the stronger it will become.

Don't Question How This Works

The act of driving your most desired goals into

your subconscious via imagination and writing them out will train your mind to seek out people and opportunities congruent with your goals. Follow this exercise up with a weekly and daily to-do list that is congruent to the goals you have put into your subconscious. Your weekly and daily to-do list is key!

Many of the items on your weekly and daily to-do list will be a natural result of the ideas and insights generated by the act of writing and re-writing your goals. Please etch firmly in your mind that it is the behaviors and motions you carry out that make all the difference. Just writing down your goals and suggesting them to yourself is not enough. You must get in motion.

You can get help training your subconscious mind

Although I don't have much of a practice, I have studied hypnosis. In hypnosis, we (the hypnotist) simply do suggestions for you. Let's say that your goal was to be free from the addiction to smoking. We'd get you into the hypnotic state and communicate to your subconscious mind how good it feels to be free from cigarettes. We can train your subconscious mind to help you reach just about any goal that you set for yourself. The beauty is that you can work this powerful principle for yourself too.

What To Do At Bed Time

Right before you fall off to sleep at night is another good time for you to train your subconscious mind. Each night relax your body and then suggest your goals to yourself in the form of affirmations. Take your goals and repeat them each a couple of times. The key again is to think or speak in the first person, present tense. You'd say; "I earn $____ per year." "I have a happy healthy family." I am a (insert title you seek)."

Other nightly affirmations could be...

"Every day in every way I am getting better and better."

"I am living my ideal life now."

"I am happy, healthy, wealthy and wise."

"I bring joy to the lives of others."

"I am physically and mentally fit."

"I am responsible with my financial affairs."

"My wealth grows each day."

"I have an excellent reputation for honesty, integrity and dependability."

"I manage my time well and maintain an equal balance of work, pleasure and family."

"I wake up energized and ready to take on the day with confidence and enthusiasm."

"I overcome any adversity and see every challenge as a learning experience."

Feel free to keep adding to this list.

The key is to constantly program your subconscious mind using the power of positive suggestion. In essence this is called "self-hypnosis." Like I said before, you can get help by also adding a good consulting hypnotist to your success plan. I am a firm believer in the "Parthenon Theory." Just like several pillars that made up the Parthenon, several pillars should support and facilitate your goals. Why not increase your odds of success by taking action, getting into motion and using some success principles that have worked for others?

Expectancy And Behavior

You need to believe in these methods and believe that your goals will be realized. Expectancy is powerful, and it can be positive or negative. This is where the area becomes gray!

I know you might have been told to "expect great things" or some other motivational saying. Many people have been disappointed because their expectations were not met. But expectancy must be combined with behavior. Let's say you wanted to get in better physical shape. If you confidently expect that you'll be successful in getting to your ideal physical condition that is great. But if your behavior is to not exercise and frequently eat fast food, then your positive expectations are being sabotaged by your behaviors.

Your behaviors must be totally in line with your goals and expectations. Writing and re-writing your goals and using the power of suggestion are not enough. But they are pillars in your Parthenon of success!

Behave as though you are living your ideal life. Do what you'd be doing. If you are looking to advance in the corporate world, begin asking for and taking on more responsibility. Take control and become a "go to" person in your organization. My wife, Jamie, received a performance based award her first year in her new position. She was one of only three people in the entire company to receive this recognition based on her performance. Please read performance as "behavior." Sure, she went into her new position with a great attitude and the best of expectations. But her secret was to get into motion quickly by behaving as a top performer.

Set your goals based on your own desires. Write them down several times per week. Say them in your mind throughout the day. And finally, engage in behaviors and take actions congruent with your goals.

Chapter 13

The Hidden Power Of The Subconscious Mind

"They can because they think they can" (Virgil)

Studying human nature is a fascinating thing. Many of us are constantly searching for the "answers to success." We are fascinated with successful people. Many books have been written that have profiled successful people. Marketers capitalize on this by promising that they have the "secrets" to success that we have been missing all of these years. Well look no further!

Beyond simply taking action, "The Success Secret That Never Fails," the answers to your success are buried in your subconscious mind. You have goals, right? You have dreams, hopes and aspirations right? We all do! But until you can convince your subconscious to accept the goal and believe in the dreams, nothing much will change.

Emotions have a whole lot to do with it too. Think about a time when your intentions were great. Maybe you started a diet to get to your ideal weight. Or maybe you began a project with the intention to see it through to completion. But you failed to follow through. Instead you ended up back in your old routines or you got distracted or tripped up and just never got the "motivation" back to get going again.

You beat yourself up trying to figure out what you did wrong. In most cases you did nothing wrong at all. What happened was the subconscious desire to return to your comfort zone won out over the conscious intention to carry out the new directions.

> "The will to survive is not the strongest instinct of the human mind. The strongest instinct of the human mind is to do what is familiar."
>
> -Virginia Satir

"I know I should go workout tonight, but 'happy hour' is so much more inviting, I can get started again next week." Then next week comes and nothing happens!

"I know I should budget time to act on this new idea I have for my business." Unfortunately, it's easier to get buried in "busy" work than to go through the pain of bringing an idea to life. Years later, someone is selling what you thought of! The difference was that they got in motion. On a side note, there's a fortune to be made simply by scrounging around the idea junkyard.

Let me give you an example of when I got an idea to introduce a new subscription program. The program was a combination of a few things, all of which were buried in my subconscious mind. The program consisted of an idea that someone else had that never got off the ground and something that I heard on a tele-seminar. It was also the answer to a question that I had posed to my subconscious mind a few weeks before getting it.

There were a few reasons why this other person could not get the idea off the ground. One was the fact that this individual seemed to have "follow-through" problems in general. The other is that the idea (the way he had it structured) had a few major flaws. His lack of action in actually getting the product done so he had something to sell was a problem too.

Get In Motion

About ten minutes after the idea and the name for it popped into my mind, I jumped out of bed at about eleven o'clock on a Thursday night, went down into my home office and registered the website domain name. I got in motion ten minutes after getting the idea! The next day, I mapped it out and then sent the concept off to my webmaster to begin working on it. Over the next week I wrote the promotional copy for the program. Then, I began offering it to my current membership subscribers as an additional service. After I proved to myself that it could be sold, I then began offering it to prospects on my email list.

A Combination of The Subconscious Mind, Motion and Belief

Information influences your mind whether you want it to or not! The example I gave you above came from the information that had been dumped into my subconscious over a certain period of time. It's just a matter of bringing it out.

That's why it is so important to give your mind quality information that it can feed back to you when you need it most. You've heard the computer slang, GIGO, right? Garbage in, garbage out! Well, we want "Good in, Good out!" You are taking in "good" right now so keep it up.

Information influences your behavior. In short, input = output. It either happens right away or eventually. But make no mistakes about it ... information influences behavior. It can be very positive too when you act on ideas that lead you closer to your goals.

Motion and belief feed off of each other. If I had not put my idea in motion the positive emotions that are caused by taking action would have never shown up. Not taking action will only undermine your belief in yourself. Think about it - if I had let days go by and not done anything with the idea, if I had not gotten into motion, my emotions would have turned negative. I would have started to say to myself, "Another idea that you didn't act on, you dreamer. Why don't you just give up and get a day job?"

Well, maybe not that harsh, but you get the point!

3 STEP SUCCESS FORMULA

Motion Creates Belief in Yourself

Belief in Yourself Creates Positive Emotions

Positive Emotions Give You The Desire To Fuel The Motivation You Need To Keep Going.

Remember - keep that flow of quality information pouring into your subconscious! Turn off the TV BEFORE you fall asleep! Get in motion when you get an idea; the market place will tell you if the idea is valid or not.

It doesn't matter what you want ... ideas for business success, a smoother personal life or to achieve your ideal weight ... the answers are buried in your subconscious mind. Ask for the answers, look for the answers and then get in motion.

If you want to give your mind the quality information you need to influence you in a positive way, be sure to check out www.askmiked.com for my latest thoughts and techniques. Be sure to sign up for my email newsletter and get a free audio called, "Get Mobilized," when you're there.

Chapter 14

How To Let Go Of "Waste"

*"Think about any attachments that are
depleting your emotional reserves.
Consider letting them go" (Oprah Winfrey)*

Dave Pelzer, a New York Times bestselling
author, compared the mind to the digestive
system. "We eat something and our digestive
system extracts the nutrients and gets rid of the
waste. Our minds are not as efficient; we tend
to hold on to a lot of mental waste that
ultimately drags us down."

Why is that?

Picture your mind as being like your PC (or
Mac). What you see on the screen is what you
are currently working on. But in the
background, there are all kinds of things going
on that affect your PC's performance. Your PC
won't be efficient when there are all kinds of
cookies, spy-ware, and other stuff that I really
know nothing about clogging up its short-term
memory and operational system. Your PC's
hard drive has a lot to do with its performance.

Your subconscious (which we explored a little earlier) is like your mental hard drive. It's what's going on in the background. Sure, your conscious mind may be at work on a particular goal or task, but if your subconscious is not accepting of the task then it will negatively impact your chances of success.

Your subconscious mind affects your daily life in a negative way by rehashing old negative wasteful thoughts. The problem is that these thoughts stir certain emotions, and your emotions tend to affect your mood and, more importantly, your behaviors.

The next time you recognize that you are dwelling on an old negative belief or thought, yell the word "STOP" (to yourself). Then, replace the negative with a positive thought of past or future success. It is critically important that you get in touch with the feelings associated with this successful thought. When you are in tune with the feelings, you will then stir up the emotions that will lead to productive behaviors.

I have found that another superb way of banishing negative thoughts is to think about something that Socrates said. It went something like: If we all were to put our problems in a heap so that we may divide them evenly, each person would be content to keep their own.

Your negative thoughts are caused when you dwell on past and current problems. Realize that past problems are now wisdom. Current problems are opportunities for future growth. Extract the nutrients from every situation, then move on. How? Just do it! Be bigger than the failure or problem. Stop wasting your time.

There Can Be A Lot Of Waste In Your Business Too

Hanging on to old ways of doing things or systems that just are not productive anymore will equal a ton of waste.

It is a great idea to look at your business and see where you can make it more efficient.

Are you producing or carrying too many products? Remember the 80/20 principle - eighty percent of your sales come from twenty percent of your products.

Apply the same rule to your customers or clients. Are some clients actually costing you time and money to keep them?

As we know: Bigger is not always better, or dinosaurs would rule the Earth. Are you hanging on to empty space? Is your office bigger than it needs to be?

Do you have inventory that has been hanging around for years? If you have a localized business then you are limited by geography. Perhaps those dusty items should be sold on eBay? Even at a loss, would you rather have cash or dusty inventory?

Many companies that struggle in economic downturns are usually carrying a lot of waste in the form of advertising that is not working and operational procedures that are inefficient and outdated. Don't believe me? Study just a few of the companies that stood in line for government handouts in recent times!

Become more efficient in your business and personal life by letting go of waste and you'll get to where you want to be so much faster.

Chapter 15

Why Simple Is Better

"The secret of success is making your vocation your vacation" (Twain)

I love the above quote because it is such a simple way to look at success.

It's really a shame that most people would go to great lengths to complicate their lives and situations. The most successful folks understand simple is better! Think about the best businesses: they're simple, easy to understand, and to the customer, they come off as clear and concise.

The best sales people know the old sales rule that says, "If you confuse 'em, you lose 'em!" They make their presentations fun and easy to follow. They make their words and sentences short and to the point. I'm reminded of a time when someone was trying to sell me insurance and mutual funds. As my eyes glazed over I remember thinking, "What is this guy talking about?" He just kept rambling on and on about the company he worked for. Boring and complicated to say the least.

Understand The Law Of Simplicity

Very few people actually practice the law of simplicity. Spouses will argue about minutia and in the process ruin an entire evening that could have been capped off with some much needed love-making. Most people will complicate their finances and overdo their "budget." Keep it simple: what you make minus what you spend to support your lifestyle. If the latter is greater than the former for too long then bankruptcy awaits! Apply the "Chunka Principle" to your finances. What is the "Chunka Principle? The chunka coming in must be bigger than the chunka going out.

Your decisions will complicate your life if you are not careful. Ask yourself if a decision you're about to make will eventually make your life simpler. Will the decision produce short-term complexity but long-term simplicity? Are you prepared to deal with the short-term complexity to achieve long-term simplicity? If the answer comes back as "Yes, it's worth it!" then go for it!

It's simpler to live in a comfortable house that you're easily making the mortgage payments on than it is to live in a "McMansion" that's making you broke. It's even easier to live in a house that's paid off!

For a while I didn't own a *Blackberry*. It broke, and I never replaced it. I just had a normal phone for two years. I saved a few bucks on the monthly bill for a while. Eventually I got an *Android* phone but only because it actually DOES simplify things. As I learned more and more about smart phones my company embraced mobile marketing. I have apps on my phone I actually use for business. Thank God for the navigation map or else I'd have been late for many speaking engagements! My sense of direction is not good – in fact, I always warn people not to follow me down the buffet line if they're hungry! I don't use my smart phone for pleasure, just business. And try not to check email or text messages while driving. Yes, broken bones and hospital stays can really complicate your life.

I like nice things and technology of course. But what does it for me are the simple things and a feeling that I'm contributing value to the world!

Put simplicity in motion in your life. You'll find that it's easier to get things done and take continuous action when things are simple. The first thing to do is to start with a mind-set that life just does not have to be so complicated.

Chapter 16

How To Deal With Stress

"You cannot prevent the birds of sorrow from flying over your head, but you can prevent them from building nests in your hair" (Chinese Proverb)

There were two attorneys coming out of a downtown office building. They both witnessed a terrible accident. A man they both knew was hit by a bus and killed instantly! One of the attorneys quickly became upset, angry, panicked and stressed. The other said, "That's sad," and then went about his business.

The man that was hit by the bus was a witness in the case they were both working on. The attorney who became instantly stressed was the prosecutor. The one who really could care less was the defense attorney. You might be laughing or you may think I'm crazy, but that story illustrates what stress is.

Stress is simply a reaction to stimuli. In the above example both these men were acted upon by the exact same stimuli, but their reactions were totally different. Stress was necessary to our survival thousands of years ago. Thousands of years ago it was known as "flight or fight." The caveman hunting for food would either run from the big saber-tooth cat or he'd stay and fight. As you can imagine, either choice would prove to be stressful.

I am neither a psychologist nor a medical doctor, and I have never played one on TV. However, I am smart enough to know that most of the stress in people's lives is brought about by no one other than themselves! Yes, I know, "Other people cause you stress!" Your kids, your co-workers, your spouse, your employees and don't forget your in-laws. It's sad how many of the people in your life who cause you stress have the same last name as you.

Stress Or Headache?

There is a difference between someone being a "headache" in your life and someone "causing you stress." People in your life who are giving you headaches can slow or altogether stop your forward motion if you allow them to do so. Keywords here: "if you allow them."

Let's face it - "stress" sells a lot pills for the big drug companies. Every so often I get a client who wants to reduce their business stress, so they hire me. What I do is help them eliminate stress from their business by implementing better marketing and selling strategies. It's amazing how much increased profits can reduce stress levels.

Headaches can usually be dealt with a little quicker. If someone or something is giving you a headache, just move on and be thankful it did not lead to real stress.

Stress is your reaction to stimuli

When my girls were younger they were very picky about their socks and shoes. The slightest bit of discomfort caused them to whine and cry. They just don't know how to deal with the discomfort caused by the clumpy sock! They knew that daddy or mommy would fix it. We had to choose our reaction. Yell, scream, break out into a sweat and demand they quit complaining. Or calmly, in a relaxed tone, ask, "What seems to be the problem sweetie?" The later always worked better. The trick was remembering to use it. You have the power to make choices about how you respond to stimuli all day long. If you're getting stressed, it is really caused by you choosing the stressful response. Take a deep breath and refer to my friend Aila Accad's book, "34 Instant Stress Busters."

The Waves

When my parents would take my brothers and I to the Jersey shore (this was before the reality show on MTV) for the day or week, visiting the beach was on the itinerary of things to do. In South Philly, we had the "black tar beach." That's the fire hydrant (a.k.a. "fire plug") and the street. As you could imagine, the real beach with the sand and waves of the was a really cool place to go. I remember asking my parents if the waves ever take a break. Not surprisingly, the response was, "Nope, they just keep coming!" And there you have it with life's problems, big or little. They just keep coming!

Ultimately, you have to decide if you want to try to battle the mighty ocean. Honestly, I'd rather learn to surf, play in the waves, ride a boogie board and just have some fun. Your problems are never going to stop coming. When your problems finally do stop, the lid will be closed. When the lid closes, you'll have more important items to worry about, like whether you're going to heaven or hell, coming back as a new baby, an animal, or an insect. Of course, you can prepare for whatever you believe and I'll prepare for what I believe.

Compared To What?

An excellent tool to reduce or totally eliminate stress from your life is to ask, "Compared to what?" Everything is relative. Success is relative. I have conveyed through these pages that if you are living the life you really want to live and working toward worthwhile goals without breaking any laws, then you are a success. Wealth is relative. Do you want to compare your wealth to Warren Buffet's wealth? Or, do you want to do your best to keep your debts low, your cash flow in good working order and save money for the future? I'd take the latter! Comparing your wealth to Warren Buffet's will only stress you out. Any problem you have is relative. The flu that kept you in bed with aches and pains is nothing compared to the agony experienced by a person who is suffering with cancer. The financial problems I had at one point in my life were nothing compared to the financial problems of the thousands of people who lost their homes to foreclosure.

I don't want you to brim with excitement when you find out that someone is worse off than you. No way! But when you begin to appreciate what you have, control your responses to stimuli and train your mind to focus on the positive, you can begin to eliminate the word stress from your vocabulary. Now don't stress, keep reading.

Chapter 17

The Gritted Teeth Theory Of Success And Why It's Total BS!

"That which we persist in doing becomes easier - not that the nature of the task has changed, but our ability to do it has increased" (Ralph Waldo Emerson)

In the beginning we talked about how when you try to push your way to success, it only pushes you back. In this chapter we'll build on that law a little more.

Of course there is a price for success, just as there's a price for failure. There's a price for everything! But when is the price not worth it? When do you throw in the towel and stop gritting your teeth, working sixteen-hour days and driving yourself crazy?

Are you a quitter if you get off of a sinking ship? The captain is supposed to go down with the ship, but that is at sea, not in life. Are you a quitter if you finally give up on a business venture that is going nowhere? Are you a quitter if you stop chasing someone else's dreams and goals and start working toward your own definition of success?

I say NO, but with a catch. If your best talents are not being utilized ... If your creative energy and emotions are drained ... If you're sick and tired of being sick and tired, then it is fine to change course and put in motion another dream or goal. Knowing when to get out does not make you a quitter. It does not make you a loser. It keeps you sane!

Success is a relative term, but there is a minimum requirement. Be realistic about your situation.

If you are living life on your terms and not effecting anyone else in a negative way, then I'd call you successful to the degree that you are happy with where you are. If you're not happy with where you are or what you're doing then you have not yet achieved success. Of course, you can be happy and keep going to achieve more success.

Success comes from using and leveraging your best talents. Those talents are in your head and heart and not in your wallet. Those talents get better and more valuable as you pursue a dream you are happy with that brings value to others. If you do not believe in the dream, that is when you'll be forced to grit your teeth, suck it up, and force yourself to be unhappy on a day-to-day basis. You'll be pushing and life will only push you back.

But I've Got Too Much Invested - I Can't Quit!

If you're on a sinking ship it doesn't matter what you've got invested - you're going to lose it all anyway. It's like the rookie day trader who thinks holding on to a bad stock will somehow make it a good stock. It's all going down. Don't be stubborn and foolish to think you can sit there with your small bucket and bail out the water. I know it is hard to justify losing your sweat, and cash, on a sinking ship, but it happens all the time and it's called the "School of Hard Knocks."

Those who graduate from the School of Hard Knocks can emerge super successful because of how valuable the education is. You can stop gritting your teeth and giving yourself premature gray hairs if you realize you can recover and will bounce back stronger than ever. As long as you get in motion quickly.

I think it's important that you don't beat up your own self-esteem if you choose an easier route to success than the one that requires gritted teeth. Usually, this will require you to do something that challenges you and keeps you sharp.

It Is Fine To Grit Your Teeth Sometimes

Now, let's give you the rules that allow for you to grit your teeth so you understand I am not just preaching, "It's okay to quit when things get difficult."

Rule Number One - It's fine to grit your teeth a little if the goals and dreams are yours wholeheartedly.

When it is your goal and your dream you can justify gritting your teeth and know your short-term pain is for long-term gain.

This also means if you've sold others on your dreams, it is up to you as a leader to keep them on track. If you sold the dream, you need to take responsibility.

Rule Number Two - Don't forget rule number one!

I'm sure you'd agree that when you engage in work that is satisfying you'll end up gritting your teeth less and less. Of course sometimes you'll have to grit those teeth to get ahead.

Chapter 18

Don't Let The Imposter Syndrome Sabotage Your Success!

"It has all been a mistake"

My friend and early mentor, John Graden, wrote a book called *The Imposter Syndrome, How to Replace Self-Doubt with Self-Confidence* and *Train Your Brain for Success.*

The book is a great story of how he battled the Imposter Syndrome and overcame it in his own life.

The Imposter Syndrome is a deep subconscious feeling you don't deserve the success you have. It is a feeling you are somehow an imposter. That you are going to be found out and exposed for the fraud that you are! He tells the story of how famous actor Paul Newman secretly harbored the fear someone was going to bust through the crowd, informing him it had all been a mistake that he did not deserve the success he had achieved and now had to go back to painting houses.

Bill O'Reilly, the famous host of the "O'Reilly

Factor" on the Fox News Channel points out in his book, *A Bold Fresh Piece of Humanity*, how many wealthy, far left liberals, harbor a deep feeling of guilt that causes them to force their views of wealth re-distribution and social responsibility on everyone who has achieved a certain level of financial success.

In the U.S, tax brackets, plus the fact many wealthy people are very charitable, help the less fortunate without the need for the government to force it. Inside they have this feeling that they don't deserve the success they've achieved. They assume everyone else must be made to feel guilty or obligated by their own success to "take care" of everyone else. Yes, there are people in our society who we need to care for. But there are a whole lot who are "cared for" who are very capable of taking care of themselves.

The imposter syndrome explains why so many lottery winners end up in the same desperate financial affairs as they were prior to winning. Deep down, their subconscious can't handle the sudden influx of cash minus all of their financial worries. Therefore, like a rubber band, they snap back into place and continue the same life with just a few extra zeros added to their financial mess. Deep down they harbor the feelings of not deserving their financial windfall.

The celebrities who have died because of their drug addictions were taken down by the Imposter Syndrome. Chris Farley, Kurt Cobain and Elvis are just a few on the list of people who accomplished amazing things in their careers and lives, then engaged in self-sabotage that led to their ultimate demise. I know of many successful entrepreneurs that lost it all after years of hard work. The key is being aware the imposter syndrome exists. Many of these same entrepreneurs rebuilt their wealth and ultimately kept it! So the imposter syndrome can be beaten.

When you get in motion and achieve the life you want and the success you desire, you must work hard to keep it going. If you earned it, you deserve it! Despite what your friends and neighbors may think. The auto-suggestive term: "Every day in every way, I am getting better and better" may be worn out, but it is an excellent tool for convincing your subconscious mind that you are worth all that you have achieved! Combine this attitude with a disdain for complacency and bias for action and you'll be all set.

Even if you inherited it, you deserve it

Have you ever wondered why so many "rich kids" go off the deep end? Well, as John Graden points out – it's the imposter syndrome at work. At the same time, so many people are jealous of those who were born into the "lucky sperm/egg club."

There are two lessons for you to take away.

1) If you are a member of the "lucky sperm/egg club," feel good about it! Give back a little if that's what your conscience is telling you to do. Stay in motion to keep the success of your family   going.

2) If you find yourself in envy of these people – get a life and get in motion to make your kids part of the lucky sperm/egg club.

For an interesting case study just compare Ivanka Trump, Donald Trump's daughter, to Paris Hilton. The perception that I get of Ivanka is she is the future of the upscale Trump brand and empire. Everything about her speaks loud and clear that she knows she is no imposter. She knows what her role is in carrying on her father's legacy. Of course, she is only human, so time will tell. On the other hand, the perception I get from Paris Hilton is one of always looking for attention in the wrong ways for the wrong reasons. It seems as though she has been conditioned to take her allowance of the family fortune and do what she wants, just so long as she stays out of the business. Again, that's just my perception. I could be wrong - I often am, just ask my wife, she'll tell you.

You can beat the Imposter Syndrome. Just remember it is not a hoax. You deserve all you have achieved and all that you will achieve.

***

Evergreen Success Principle

You're Not Defeated Unless You Accept Defeat

There really is no losing or failure in life if you learn from every experience and every mistake. Remember these words...

"Whatever doesn't kill me makes me stronger."

***

Chapter 19

Are The Little Things Holding You Back?

"Little hinges swing big doors" (Dan Kennedy)

My wife and I fight! (Not physically - she would kick my butt.) In the beginning. we'd let it get to us, mostly because my mother or her mother would say "You two fight too much!" Then we saw the movie *The Notebook*, and I know it may seem silly, but those two lovebirds fought a lot too. However, they decided to get used to it. We don't let it bother us. The kids know that mommy and daddy are never going to be in agreement on everything. They understand that sometimes adults raise their voices to negotiate differences of opinion and to make themselves heard. If we didn't see our arguments as a natural part of life, we might have given up on each other. We also make sure that we show our kids how much we love each other by hugging and showing affection in front of them.

Do Sweat The Small Stuff

I don't subscribe to the whole "Don't sweat the small stuff" philosophy, because what is small to you might be enormous to someone else. I am really domestically challenged. I try my best though. I load the dishwasher, I take out the garbage and I carry down laundry. I really don't enjoy doing any of these activities. I don't take pride in doing them either. And if doing them right and getting them done are not the same thing, then they are not going to always be done right. Jamie really does try to point out to me how I am supposed to load the dishwasher. And I am getting better, really. I do, however, understand that getting it done right is important to her, so I make my best effort to do things the way she wants them done. But here's the funny thing...

I view all of these tasks as life's minor inconveniences. If you are less than super wealthy and don't have a kitchen and house staff like the Banks family in the Disney classic *Mary Poppins*, then you will have to deal with these things. Jamie and I actually agree they are small things - but she makes note of the fact that when she asks me to do them a certain way to please her is not a small thing. I think she's got a point. And there you have the difference of opinion. So we simply compromise. She understands I don't have a domestic bone in my body, but she still expects me to hold up my end with some quality and attention to details when I do these tasks. I understand she is a busy woman and does not have time to get everything done exactly to her liking on the home front. Therefore, it is my job to adapt and contribute my extra energy to help the household flow smoother. Together we make a good team. Of course our cleaning, lawn care and snow removal services help too!

Bottom line ... we both hold up our ends of the deal to the best of our abilities, and even though our opinions differ on "small things," we make it work because we understand each other.

In Business

When someone tries to grow a business, it is usually the small things that trip him up. Many business owners simply pay attention to the wrong things. They get too hung up in the day-to-day and technical sides of things that they forget to market and sell their services.

In business, especially if you are just starting out, you must allocate a set amount of time each day to find new clients and customers. Unfortunately, many business owners get so caught up in the "job" of what they are doing they forget to market. Let's say your friend has a carpet cleaning business. In early November, he begins getting calls from customers who want their carpets cleaned before their holiday gathering. So he books himself solid beginning the week before Thanksgiving through Christmas. Then he fulfills his obligations and come January 1st his calendar is empty for the next week. At first he welcomes the downtime. But then no calls come in the whole week! Now next week is looking slow. In a panic, he begins calling customers and booking appointments, and then the cycle repeats. All the while, he just tells himself how happy he'd be if his business were just "steady."

If your friend, the carpet cleaner, would take care of some important "little things," like implementing a system to book the next cleaning while he was finishing the current cleaning job he wouldn't have been in a panic. He could have simply told the customer, "Mr. Jones, I know you are getting your carpets cleaned because of your upcoming holiday gatherings, right?" The customer would respond, "Yes!" Then he'd be able to say, "Well, I am not sure how many people you are expecting but it'd probably be a good idea to schedule your next cleaning now for right after the holidays so we can deep clean after all that traffic comes through. Would you want to go for the week after Christmas or the week after the 1st of January?" See, a little thing that would spell the difference between being booked steady or hoping the phone rings.

I have never worked in a corporate office, but I do know plenty of people who have. I know in the corporate world moving up the ladder is sometimes the measurement of success. The vast majority of people who work in a corporate environment would probably tell you they are trying to climb the ladder. I mean, come on, who would admit they have no desire to move up? The sad thing is while the majority will profess to being upwardly mobile, the majority will also engage in activities that sabotage their own success. What's even more amazing is it will be the little things that hold them back.

The Crazy Phenomenon About "Little Things" Is Some Of Them Matter And Some Of Them Don't!

If you send your significant other a love note every once in a while, that's a little thing that can have a huge impact. When you write business associates and clients thank you notes – that's a little thing, but it sets you apart because it rarely gets done. Returning phone calls or emails in a timely manner is a little thing. Remembering someone's name is a little thing that matters. See, most "little things" that matter and make a positive difference in your life and the lives of others usually require just a bit of effort. The effort is totally worth it.

Broken Windows And "Squeegee Men"

After the real estate boom of 2003 through 2006, the U.S. housing market took a nosedive. Foreclosures jumped as cash-strapped homeowners who got in over their heads went delinquent on their payments. Imagine, just for a second, that one of those foreclosed properties happened to be in your neighborhood. Of course, it will negatively impact the value of your home. But, just for minute, think about what would happen if while the house sat vacant, a group of vandals decided to break one of the windows? Then, since a bank owned the house, the window never got fixed. One broken window may seem like no big deal, but that "little thing" could snowball. If that happened in your neighborhood, it would be best for you to show up at the bank's corporate office and demand they fix that window. Why? Because studies have proven that criminals see the one neglected broken window in the neighborhood as a sign that they could get away with more serious crimes.

Mayor Rudolph Giuliani cleaned up New York City during his years as mayor. He went after small things aggressively (of course he went after bigger things like murder as well). He knew that quickly removing graffiti from the subway would boost morale amongst the millions of hard-working people who used it for transportation. The stronger moral for the majority led to the rides becoming safe again. He issued citations for jay walking. Many major intersections of the city were over-run with "Squeegee Men." These men would clean your car windows and then demand payment. For many tourists, this was their first "tourist attraction" as they entered the Big Apple. He arrested many of them for extremely minor infractions. Come to find out, most of the "Squeegee Men" were actually hardcore criminals with outstanding arrest warrants.

Now you know that "don't sweat the small stuff" is a false theory. Everything is relative. What is small to you may be enormous to someone else. Small things left unchecked can slow your forward motion and even set you back.

See The BIG Picture

You've heard that before, right? It seems as though the idea of "Seeing the BIG picture" and not worrying about little things is a common theme. I agree that you must see the BIG picture. Of course, you know people who are shortsighted, flaky, small-time thinkers just can't see the big picture. They can't see how their actions (or lack thereof) affect their lives down the road. When a business takes your money and then doesn't deliver as promised, it is missing the big picture. When the business doesn't own up to the fact that they did not deliver, it may appear as though the business has won. On the contrary, they have lost! The inability to see the big picture and understand that repeat customers are the key to success in business will do them in eventually.

In Order For You To Be Successful You Must See The Big Picture AND Take Care Of The Little Things That Matter!

On a personal note...

Let's say you have this great vision of your ideal family life. It is perfect in every way. The family is happy, successful, healthy, and there's an abundance of love flowing. Part of your vision and one of the reasons you are happy is because you are financially free. In the capitalist system financial freedom usually provides you with more options. No doubt, to be financially free requires work. The mistake that people make is that they see the work as something that will come before happiness. It should really be a part of your happiness. Can you really tell yourself that you'll be happy when some condition causes you to be happy? "I'll be happy when I build my business up and then could take more time off to be with my family." Bad idea! That day might never come. Sure, you might build your business up, but how do you know when enough is enough? You really need to enjoy the ride. The fun of success is the chase. Success does not cause happiness.

"What Is Happiness?"

According to an article in *Psychology Today*, "The most useful definition - and one that is agreed upon by neuroscientists, psychiatrists, behavioral economists, positive psychologists and Buddhist monks – is that it is closer to satisfaction or contentment rather than 'happiness' in its strict bursting-with-glee sense. It has depth and deliberation to it. It encompasses living a meaningful life, utilizing your gifts and your time, living with thought and purpose."

I shared that definition of happiness with you because I like it as a "Big Picture" definition of happiness. Living a meaningful life involves paying attention to important "little things" and ignoring or minimizing less meaningful "little things."

With little things you must choose your battles carefully. Some little things will not contribute much at all to your goals and happiness. Some little things will actually slow your forward motion. On the other hand, paying attention to certain "little things" and actually performing them well will do more to propel you forward than anything else.

Chapter 20

Small Minds, Medium Minds And Big Minds

"Little things affect little minds"(Benjamin Disraeli)

I originally heard this brilliant concept of small, medium, and big minds from a great martial-arts instructor named Tom Callos. Your words and actions are a direct result of what's going on in your mind. We know that our outer world is a direct reflection of our inner world combined with the action we take each day. It's kind of like a circle that just keeps rotating.

When you hear someone gear their outer conversation toward talking about other people in a negative way, you know that they are in the "small mind" category! If you think about it, what can be accomplished by simply talking about others in a negative way? I know, there's a certain amount of entertainment value, and some folks get paid the big bucks to actually sit there and do this. But relative to all the folks who get paid big bucks to talk about others in a negative way, there are millions of broke, miserable, and downright UN-happy people who go about their day-to-day lives talking about others. These folks have small minds and small minds talk about people most of the time.

When you hear someone's conversations and general topics of discussion geared towards things. Material possessions like houses, cars, clothes, watches, etc. - they are in the medium mind category. Medium minds are, most of the time, fixated on "things." The medium-minded individual will spend time surfing the net for "stuff" to buy.

Buying a new car is a monumental event for these people. The problem with having a medium mind is that it's never satisfied. Think about it - if you're constantly fixated on "stuff," will the obsession ever go away? Will you ever have enough?

Finally - "Big Minds"

Big minds are the minds that make things happen! They're the minds that bring great ideas to life and move the world forward. Get around some very successful folks and the gist of their conversations will be that of "what's next" and "what idea are we bringing to life?" Big minds talk about ideas! They have little time for any other useless thoughts because they are usually in motion working on their ideas.

I know you are moving toward the category of "big mind," so please, let your conversations and thoughts be that of ideas for your life and career that you are bringing into reality. Yes, of course you'll get caught up every now and then talking about someone. Just don't overdo it and you'll be fine. I do my best to catch myself, and then I say, "that's enough" - in my own mind of course.

Chapter 21

Get Rid Of The People Who Slow You Down

"Respond intelligently even to unintelligent treatment" (Lao Tsu)

Unfortunately, there are people in your life who will act as the force that slows your forward motion. The good news is that your gut feelings enable you to quickly identify these motion stoppers. The sad truth is the "gut feeling" someone is slowing you down is usually not enough to change anything. You must get in motion to eliminate these people from your life.

The people who kill your forward motion come in so many varieties. They can be brothers, sisters, parents, friends, co-workers and in-laws. Their weapons of choice can be blame, guilt, addiction, physical or mental abuse or manipulation. Other people can sabotage your success if you let them.

I told you the story earlier about how my mother-in-law just could not appreciate the fact that Jamie and I took her in and provided for her when she needed it most. Sure, she could have gone to the government for help with housing and keeping food in her stomach, and the system would have taken care of her sooner rather than later. But we offered and she accepted.

It took us a long time to realize what a force of negativity she actually was. Our marriage was held back. At a critical time our finances were pressured more than they should have been. And our forward motion toward our goals was constantly being held back by "the week's disagreement." The weapons of choice were guilt. "After all, I am your mother." And manipulation. "Well, who is going to take care of Julia and Marissa while you both are working?"

Remember, you are not obligated to anyone who is making your life miserable even if they have the same last name or maiden name as you. As I told you earlier, the world is abundant! When you make a decision to disassociate with people who are holding you back, both your life and (sometimes) their life will get better. Jamie's mother got her act together to a certain degree after we made the split. Of course, there was some damage done to the relationship between mother and daughter, but it was a necessary price to pay.

You Make the Choice

When I was a teenager, there were two huge forces that kept me away from drugs while many of the kids in my neighborhood were doing them. One force was my martial arts training. I earned my black belt in Taekwondo right before my sixteenth birthday. After that, I got involved in Brazilian Jiu-Jit-Su. When I was eighteen I was operating my own small martial arts school. I quickly became a responsible adult (in some ways) and therefore really had no time for the whole "experimental" phase that most kids go through.

The other major force keeping me away from drugs in a neighborhood that was frankly overrun with them was seeing how drugs destroyed most of my brother's early adulthood. He wrecked cars and couldn't hold down a job or girlfriend. It really was horrible to watch someone I loved and once looked up to battle an addiction that was destroying his life and the lives of the people around him. And that leads me to another example of how others will take you down with them if you let them.

I hope I never have to go through with either of my daughters what I witnessed my parents go through with my brother. His drug addiction taxed their lives emotionally, physically and financially. My father would have to get out of bed at all hours of the night due to something that my brother was doing. My brother would fall asleep with candles burning. He would have every light in the house turned on at three in the morning. He would have the television blasting throughout the night. I knew it had gotten bad when he began to smoke his marijuana in my parents' house.

For me it was just a matter of ignoring it. I could tell my parents what I thought they should do, but ultimately it was up to them. I'd spend most of my day out of the house anyway. I'd work seven days a week, six at my martial arts school and Saturday and Sunday at one of the part time jobs I had for many years. When I wasn't working, I was with my friends or with a girl I was seeing at the time. When Jamie and I started dating, every other weekend, I'd drive to North Jersey to see her. Actually, by that time my brother had cleaned up his act. I was so happy and proud of him. This was how he did it…

Finally my parents had enough! One winter, in the middle of February, they kicked him out of their house on a very cold night. My brother once told me he didn't remember much from that night except for waking up and being surprised he was still alive. A day later, he qualified for a top-of-the-line rehab program in Florida. The happy ending is that he got his life together and broke free of his drug addiction.

Please keep in mind the above story I told you was only to illustrate a point. I didn't tell you this so that you'd be mad at my brother, or worse, to put myself above anyone. That's not how I operate.

You have to remember you cannot help anyone who is not willing to help himself. I know there is a strong feeling of guilt and obligation that accompanies the bond of family. Addiction is dangerous for everyone in its path. If you are living with someone or close to someone who is battling an addiction, you have to realize you cannot help them. They must help themselves – the same way my brother did. And this goes for anyone who is slowing you down.

Leopards Don't Change Their Spots (most of the time)

When you buy a car and want to finance it, they run a credit check on you. Why? Because past behavior is a great indicator of future behavior. If someone is causing you grief in your life, it's a safe bet that they will continue to cause you grief. I know, you think I am being negative, but no! You either have to get used to them and decide that you are fine with it, or take some action. My parents by default (lack of doing something about it for so many years) decided that they wanted to live within the nightmare of my brother's addictions. For them to think things would change without them taking drastic measures was a fantasy. The more drastic the motion is, the more drastic and faster the reactions will come.

What will keep you sane and in motion is to *assume* that the people who are slowing you down will continue to slow you down. Therefore, your only logical choice is to get them out of your life. When you make that decision they will be forced to make the important decision of helping themselves! And sometimes you'll be able to actually welcome them back into your life because they have changed.

The "People Don't Change" Attitude Is Helpful In Business Too

I told you how I really got myself into a couple of sticky business situations. In both cases, the people I was dealing with had repeated past behavioral patterns.

When I was involved with the unproductive business relationship, there was this one guy who worked for them who had done some flaky things.

In business, you are flaky when you...

1) Are late without notice or a courtesy call
2) Can't seem to remember dates and times
3) Can't honor deadlines set by you or others
4) Don't return important phone calls
5) Don't return important emails in a timely manner
6) Are generally unprepared and you can't hide it

And don't worry, we all mess up - you're not flaky if you were late a few times or missed some deadlines. It's the people who do it all the time who are the problem!

The funny (but expensive) thing was I spotted the flakiness before I proceeded with the deal (shame on me). The flakiness seemed to get worse as time went on. Actually it really did not get worse. For the flaky guy it was the same all along. He was just doing what he had always done. When you get closer to someone in a relationship, their flaws become more obvious.

More Leopards Who Don't Change

When I sold a business, I couldn't operate anymore. I knew the new owner had a sketchy past. My choices were limited at the time due to a debacle I had with a previous employee. This guy (the new owner) had closed two other similar businesses. Part of me hoped that the third time would be a charm and part of me knew it really wouldn't be. Guess what - the third time wasn't a charm and he drove the business into the ground.

My guess was he was a degenerate gambler. I came to that conclusion when during our brief partnership two mysterious charges from Atlantic City showed up on my Amex card. Of course he "knew nothing about them." Shortly after he made his first installment to buy the business, he bounced several checks. I knew because the bank still had my address on file. I had an equipment vendor call me looking for payment on a C.O.D. order. Luckily they understood what was going on and contacted him for payment. In the end he remained congruent with his past. The landlord filed for eviction, and I never received full payment for the business. No regrets though, because this guy was actually very helpful in quickly getting me out of a sticky situation where my options were very limited. And yes, I learned more about reading people in the process. I can apply my wisdom to future human transactions.

Here's The Take Away...

When he finally stopped paying and was then out of my life, I easily replaced the income that he took with him when he went delinquent on the purchase of the business. And guess what. I didn't even bother to pursue him for the balance. When you get someone out of your life who is holding you back – that's it, over and done with! I guess this is an area of life where "burning bridges" will help you. Why hold on and throw good time, money and energy into seeking "retribution?"

Of course, there are circumstances when you must invest the time and money in getting a little justice. You just have to weigh the pros and cons of going through such motions. I figured I'd easily get a win against him in court but I'd have to travel six hours or pay an attorney. What for? So that I could be added to the ever-growing list of people who have court judgments against him? No thanks!

The Short-Term Pain Is Worth It

Losing money in business dealings is nothing like the pain a family member can inflict on you. They are two different kinds of pain. In business the greatest lessons are very expensive. In your personal life, you can only bring joy to those that can also bring joy to themselves.

When you make the decision to get rid of someone who is really sucking the life out of you and holding you back, it may be painful at first. Without knowing it, you might have created some sort of delusional dependency. It could be monetary or emotional. But as my friend, John Graden, says numerous times in his wonderful book *The Imposter Syndrome*, "Short term pain for long term gain."

And if you want to help them before you get rid of them...

Always remember that you can help anyone as long as they are already committed to helping themselves. If you undertake the challenge of helping someone in need, you have to make it a fifty-fifty deal and a two-way street. You'll say, "If you want my help, here's what you'll have to do for it." If they agree via their words and actions, great. Remember too. When I say "get rid of someone," what I mean is to stop allowing them to hold you back – this could mean that you really avoid contact for a while and it could also mean that you mentally make up your mind to move forward. I don't mean "whack 'em" and put them in a trunk somewhere!

The two-way street applies to business too

When I do consulting for marketing, sales and Internet marketing I put powerful systems in place for my business-owner clients. I help them with their marketing plans and campaigns. I help them simplify their lives and businesses so that they can make more money and have more time to enjoy it. But if they don't (to use a football analogy) carry the ball over the goal line, they will not score. I do my best to make it clear that I can help them implement many of the key aspects for growth in their business while I explain that ultimately their success is up to them

When You Do Get Someone Out Of Your Life You Must Get Into Motion Quickly

If you sit there and ponder what you just did, then you'll allow your feelings of guilt or the craving for what is familiar to override the good decision you have just made. You'll end up giving that person "just one more chance." - "I'll give you one more chance" is usually a bad idea. If you end a personal relationship, do your best to get around some supportive friends. Take up a new hobby. Crack the cover of a new book. Take a vacation by yourself. Do something to alter the routine. Before Jamie and I began dating, she actually ended a relationship that was going nowhere. She changed the locks at her apartment in North Jersey, drove 100 miles to visit with some friends for a few days, and when she returned to North Jersey, she began salsa dancing five nights a week in New York City. She got in motion quickly!

If you fire a poisonous employee, just move on. Suck it up and perform their tasks for a while. If you've been building up some "bench strength" and have people that you have already interviewed ready to go, bring someone in quickly on a probationary period. If you let the terminated employee's tasks go undone or wait forever to replace him, you'll only hurt yourself.

The strategy of removing anyone from your life who slows or stops your forward motion must be applied to your business and personal life. You must look inside and be honest with yourself too.

Important Question...

Are you slowing anyone else down? If so, consider how you can ease up and let go of the individual you are holding back. It works both ways.

***

Evergreen Success Principle

Don't Blame Anyone

"When you have one finger pointed at somebody else you have three pointing right back at you."

Take full responsibility for your life and the decisions you have made.

***

Chapter 22

Are Material Things Holding You Back?

"I'd rather invest my money in knowledge and experiences than accumulate a bunch of 'things'"
(Mike D.)

Let's first get it out on the table that material things are good. There is certainly nothing wrong with striving to have the latest and greatest. There is no reason to feel guilty if you possess more or better material things than someone else. After all, you did earn it, right? I am not a huge fan of material things. But I am not advocating that we all go live in the wilderness away from modern conveniences and products that make our lives easier and better. However, you need to be careful that the need for material possessions doesn't control you and make your life more complicated than need be.

I remember my first day of "macro-economics" at the community college of Philadelphia. The instructor started off by singing a verse from the Rolling Stones, "I can't get no satisfaction, and I try and I try and I try and I try." Needless to say a majority of the urban youth sitting in that classroom in 1999 really weren't "Stones' Fans," but most knew the song.

His point was that the world of economics always has a craving for more. That's why if you try to satisfy yourself with material possessions, you will fall short every time. The real key is to not let the craving for more and better material possessions run your life. I had a conversation once with a gentleman who hadn't owned a TV in many years. That may seem to be a little extreme to you because you know people who have TVs in every room of the house!

From a sound financial standpoint, the problem with most consumer purchases is that they lose their value very quickly. If you end up not having any use for the purchase, it's not like you can liquidate it and recover your money.

If it weren't for paper and "things," the word clutter would not exist. Too many things will certainly clutter the house somewhat, in the same way that too much paper clutters the desk. Many people pay large sums of money each month to store excess items. It's amazing that people will spend $1200 per year to store $600 worth of stuff. The storage industry is happy every time a pack rat is born.

The Big Ticket Items

Anything that has a price tag upwards of $1,000 would be a "big ticket item." The lesson is to buy what you really can afford. You can either pay cash for that brand new state-of-the-art refrigerator, or profit from their "Zero Percent" credit offer by paying it off in the allotted time. Never under any circumstances should you run up long-term debts to pay for consumer spending.

The Cars

The question to answer is this - are you buying the expensive car for yourself or for someone else? Meaning, are you looking to turn heads or have the best car in the neighborhood? If so, you must reconsider your thoughts on buying certain types of cars. After all, a car is really just a tool to get you from one place to the next. As long as it is safe for you and your family – what is the big deal? Bottom line - if you struggle to make your car payment each month you are not going to be happy. You'll just be mad at yourself for not having the self-discipline to delay your gratification for a time when the expensive car wouldn't put a dent in your wallet. I had a neighbor in Philly who had two cars repossessed and one that was mysteriously firebombed in the middle of the night. I guess he never could control the urge to go out and buy a car he could not afford. I know that some professionals, say financial planners, need "the image" of a fancy car. But I think as long as your car is not horrible looking, with the tailpipe dragging along with a trail of black smoke you'll be fine. You can respect someone who drives a "modest" automobile, rather than one that empties their wallet.

The House

I guess the years of boom followed by bust in the residential real estate market taught us not to get in over our heads when it comes to a mortgage. With that said, I do believe that if you are going to splurge somewhere (and you could afford it), your house should be it. If you can comfortably afford to buy a nice house in a great neighborhood, then go for it. You deserve it! The same rules apply though - don't be mad about writing that check each month!

The Difference Between Art And Function

Many years ago, an awesome martial arts instructor explained that the fancy movements of some martial arts styles were simply that - "art." He mentioned that these moves had no application in an actual self-defense situation. He went on to mention that there are a few moves in the arts that are totally "functional." It is the functional moves that will save your life in an altercation.

In your life, some of your possessions will be art and some will be function. The art is for your appreciation, not for you to keep up with the Jones.' The function items will help you in your life. It's really going to be up to you if you want the function items to be art too. If you own a Rolex watch, you can say that the watch is a functional item. It keeps you from being late. You can also argue that it is art too because of its price tag and beauty. The key is to be responsible in your acquisition of material possessions. Remember that "You really can't get no satisfaction!" So trying to is useless!

Here are a couple more thoughts on this...

Cash is easy to manage and it provides you the freedom to do whatever you want. Before you part with it, ask yourself if you'd rather give up your cash and your freedom, or do without the item you're looking to buy. Then, invest your money. Don't simply spend it! When you buy a book, you are investing. When you buy something that could give you returns, you are investing. Think of ways you could invest rather than spend.

If you are going to spend – spend wisely. *eBay* and *Craigslist* can be great places to find deals. Learn their ins and outs and use them carefully. You'll also be surprised at how many people will actually buy your unwanted material things through these services. Jamie has done many inexpensive and wonderful Christmas holidays for our girls via eBay.

Give your unwanted items away if it makes you feel good. Jamie has been in several weddings over the years. Unfortunately, those dresses usually get worn only once! The local high school has this really cool program where she can donate her unwanted dresses to girls who would otherwise miss their proms because they can't afford a dress. Search the Internet in your area to see if you can unload your unwanted items for a good cause. It really does feel good to give away stuff you do not need anymore.

Chapter 23

Is Your Past Slowing You Down?

"Your past has been forgiven" (The Bible)

I was sitting in a seminar once listening to a guy named Bob Alexander. He said something that I will never forget. He said that many people go through life angry about their past. He went on to say that when you are angry about the past, you are often scared of the future, and that causes you to be paralyzed in the present.

The current motion of your life will shape your future. The key words are "current" and "motion." It's what you are doing now that matters. What you did in the past has led you to where you are.

You really only have control over a few things. You can control your current thoughts and you can control your current behaviors. Your thoughts will influence your current behaviors. Action-oriented thoughts are key.

Where Does The Past Live?

Right! It lives only in your mind. Therefore, you can only think about it to re-live it. Remember that your thoughts influence your current behavior and the way you feel. So why do the vast majority of people constantly re-think negative situations from their pasts? I don't know! But I do know when you dwell on negative situations from the past, you stir up the negative emotions of those moments. Those emotions affect you in the current moment and influence your behavior in a negative way. The sayings "It's not where you're from, it's where you're at" and "It's not where you've been, but where you're going" may be old but they are very applicable to taking action on your goals.

Lessons Learned From Past Failures

"Experience is not what happens to a man; it is what a man does with what happens to him" - Aldous Huxley

Some of your negative thoughts may be spurred by past mistakes and failures. These may be business or personal mistakes.

A successful person looks at every failure as an opportunity to learn a valuable lesson. The lesson is then applied to subsequent situations.

The individual who possesses common sense does not make the same mistake twice! If you are not careful, however, you can end up in the same predicament. That is why it is so important to catalog the lessons you've learned from past mistakes. When looked upon in this regard it's really not a failure. It is a successful and necessary building block on our way to reaching your goals.

Simple Exercise

To transform your past failures into valuable assets easily, you just have to recall three of them. If you can't think of three, good for you! But if you can, write them down on the lines below or a separate sheet of paper.. Next to them, write down the lessons learned that could be applied to future situations.

Past Mistake	Lesson Learned
Not doing due diligence before a major business decision	Be careful to rush into future business relationships

Use this exercise as other "hard lessons" pop into your mind from time to time. Turn those past regrets, bad decisions, and behaviors you're not proud of into valuable lessons that will help you create the future you want.

Re-frame your thoughts on past failures and begin to see them as necessary stepping-stones that have shaped who you are. Jamie frequently reminds me that all things happen for the best. Our belief is that when you are driven by goals and stay in motion, all things do happen for the best.

Chapter 24

Change is Motion

"Life is not a static thing. The only people who do not change their mind are incompetents in asylums who can't and those in cemeteries" (Everett Dirksen)

When you begin to think about the concept of getting in motion, you will no doubt find yourself facing the fact that you'll have to make some changes.

Your body repairs itself every night when you are sleeping. You are physically in a constant state of change. Your subconscious mind takes in new information every day that ultimately influences your behavior. Seasons change, months change, weeks change, days change and seconds change. Time is the measurement of change. Whether you like it or not, the one thing that is certain is change.

What's interesting is that people are resistant to change. Old habits, beliefs and ways of doing things don't give up without a fight. If you are going to accomplish something you've never accomplished before, you're going to have to engage in behaviors and activities you've never engaged in before.

If you ever find yourself wanting things to be "the way they used to be," watch out! That mindset is a sure sign that you'll end up in trouble.

Unfortunately, most people resist change. In order to make the positive *changes* in your life you must begin moving in the direction of your goals. In this case motion may represent working more, working less, changing your routine, changing jobs or ending a personal relationship.

There Are Two Sides To The Coin Of Change...

The side of the coin that you can control and the side of the coin that you can't control!

You will have a miserable time in life if you place too much emphasis on the wrong side of the coin. The side of the coin that you can't control is neither the positive nor negative side - it's the neutral, unbiased side. It does not discriminate. It simply exists. The only thing you can control when it comes to that side of the coin is your response to it.

The side of the coin of change that you can

control is like your very own destiny paintbrush. If you have a paintbrush in your hand that is full of paint, you could either touch up the room, re-paint the room a new color or make a mess! The choice is yours because you are in control of what you do with the brush. The good news is that if you don't like the results, you can choose to apply a new color or design. But make no mistake about it ... you ARE in control.

You have to be careful because some of the choices you make in your life cannot be simply painted over. Eventually, you can put the results of decisions that did not work out the way you would have liked behind you. The ripple effect (that is for how long and to what degree the decision affects your life) is magnified when the change is more significant. And the ripple effect of decision can be positive or negative, depending on what results came from your decision to make a change. I have committed to only going for positive ripple effects. It does not always work!

Both Types Of Change Can Happen Fast

The best way to communicate to you how both types of change can happen very quickly is to give a brief time-line of my own life. I have chosen to use the holiday season as a simple way to point out how things were different each year for Jamie and I. You'll be able to see what we managed to control and what simply happened.

Jamie and I met in 2002 and started dating in the late summer of 2003. During the holiday season of 2003 we spent Christmas Eve at her parents' house in Spring Lake, New Jersey. On Christmas day, we made the one hour and twenty minute drive south on the Garden State Parkway to spend the day and have dinner with my family at my oldest brother's house, which was in Bringantine right near Atlantic City. After dinner we drove a little more than two hours back up the Parkway to spend a couple of quiet days at Jamie's apartment in North Jersey. We then headed to Philadelphia, where I lived, to spend New Year's Eve with friends and ring in 2004.

Fast-forward one year later to the holidays of 2004, and there are now three of us - Jamie, Julia and Me! Julia was barely two months old when she celebrated her first Christmas. Talk about how things have changed! If you would've told us a year before that we'd be spending the next holiday season as new parents, we would have told you that you were crazy. We did talk about having kids "down the road." It just so happened that down the road for us was within a year.

A year later, during the holidays of 2005, the three of us celebrated Julia's second holiday season while Marissa, was on her way. That was also the last Christmas that Jamie would spend with her father; he passed away in August of the following year at the age of sixty. Marissa was born two months before he died.

The four of us celebrated our first holiday season together in 2006. That year was the year that Jamie and I (not knowing it totally at the time) got into the very unproductive business relationship I told you about before. We also moved out of Philadelphia and were celebrating our first Christmas in our new house.

The holiday season of 2007 ended up being the last holiday season that we would spend in that house. I was out of the unprofitable business relationship and beginning to recover from the setbacks. In the October of 2007, Jamie decided that it was time to resume her career and grabbed the opportunity that brought us to New Hampshire. As crazy as she was, she also picked out and purchased (although closing was still a month away) our new home. As most married men will tell you, "You're most likely going to live in the house your wife chooses!" The stressful part was that our current home had not been sold yet. We paid two mortgages until April of 2008 when we closed on the sale of the New Jersey house. I was transitioning from being in my martial arts studio full-time to my new business, so I welcomed the fresh start and new challenges.

The holidays of 2008 marked the first holiday season in our new home. The choices we made and the changes we accepted gave us the best results we could have hoped for.

When you look at the time-line, it may amaze you or bore you if your life has been filled with more changes.. The point of sharing it with you is to help you see which sides of the coin were at work there. The key point to take away is to always remember to:

1) Respond in an optimistic way to change that you did not expect or orchestrate.
2) Respond in a positive and action-oriented way to changes that you did put into action but did not go the way you had hoped.
3) Trust yourself to embrace the changes that will put you closer to your life's most desired goals!

***

Evergreen Success Principle

Belief In Yourself Will Attract Others Who Believe In You

To achieve your greatest success you are going to need the cooperation of other people. It may be your family, your spouse or a whole team or organization. Whether your success will take the cooperation of just one other person or a whole country of people, you're going to need them to believe in you! It doesn't matter how hard you try to get others to believe in you – if you don't believe in yourself, other people who can help you will not be attracted to you.

Years ago a guy named Glenn Turner said in a very power speech: "Today we have instant coffee, instant tea and instant dis-belief in ourselves." Nowadays it might go... "We have instant messaging, instant access, instant approval and instant dis-belief in ourselves."

Busting those limiting self-beliefs is a battle you face every day. Getting in motion and taking some action toward your goals will fuel your self-belief. Simple truth: when you move toward your goals you'll feel better about yourself!

***

Chapter 25

How To Dump Out Those Ideas And Profit From Them

"Imagination is more important than knowledge" (Albert Einstein)

As the famous Earl Nightingale said, "Ideas are like slippery fish." Ideas always pop in and out of our minds. Some, unfortunately, get lost forever. Others get scrapped because they are just not sound. The rest should be acted upon! As you begin your motion toward the life you want, you'll be the recipient of numerous ideas. They will pop into your mind when you least expect them to.

I want to introduce you to a really fun way to clear your head of ideas while also ensuring that you don't lose any good ones. Get a notebook and label a tab "Ideas." From now on, all of your ideas will go here. Get into the habit of having your notebook in reach. If having it within reach is simply not possible, use a recorder or smaller notepad and transfer the ideas later. You can also set up a account with *Google Voice*. Then, when you get an idea you can all and leave yourself a message. The message will be transcribed and emailed to you.

By getting into the habit of jotting down your ideas, you are preventing your mind and idea-generation powers from getting jammed. Basically, if you don't capture the idea and record it outside of your mind two things will happen - You will lose the idea and you will "jam up" your idea-generating device.

Think of this exercise and habit as having a "net" to capture your ideas.

Simply write down any ideas that you've had in the past. They could be what you think are the craziest, or what you think may be the "next big thing." It doesn't matter! All that matters is that you get them out of your mind and on to a sheet of paper so you can free up your idea-generating device to keep working efficiently. You'll find new and brilliant ideas will flow better than ever before.

Next

Take action on the ideas you feel good about. Get some feedback from people who are supportive, but also truthful. It makes no sense to run your ideas by your "yes man." Take one step to begin, keep it simple. I got the idea for this book based on so many conversations with people who were successful that basically said to me, "I just do it!" I started to put the pieces together and then got the idea for the concept and the first iteration of a title. Then I simply began writing. And here's another big take away... The first version of this book that was put out and made the Amazon best seller list was not perfect in my mind (and I'm sure some other people's minds too) but it was helpful to a lot of the initial readers.

Stop being "Immobilized" when it comes to your ideas. Dump them out and do something.

Chapter 26

How Unfinished Tasks Can Kill Your Forward Motion

"Nothing is so fatiguing as the eternal nagging on of an uncompleted task" (William James)

I love starting new projects. At any one time I'll have a bunch of things going on. Most entrepreneurs, especially before maturity, will suffer from this positive addiction. The time an entrepreneur matures is when the fruits of their labor and the seeds they have planted begin to grow into something beautiful. Until then, it is a little messy! Of course, the resilient entrepreneur never slows down. The good news is that most future projects end up as expansion with improvements to whatever is already in place. In the beginning, it's almost as if they are going in a thousand different directions.

Whether you would consider yourself an entrepreneur or not, you must still develop the habit of seeing your tasks to completion. A productive habit for you is to quickly identify which projects are unproductive and cross them off of your list.

An ever-growing to-do list, filled with incomplete projects that have been lingering around for a while, can be a major source of stress. Many people, especially men, are driven to closure and become very uptight when there is no end in sight. When a task or project comes to completion there is a great natural high generated. On the other hand, if you know that you are neglecting important tasks and projects there is a corresponding low that goes with it. The main issue is that "highs" keep you in motion and "lows" slow you down and cause you to expend more energy to get back in motion.

There are really two disciplines that will help you consistently "get the high" to keep you in motion, and keep you free from the stress of nagging unfinished tasks. They are goal-setting and delegation. When you have goals that are written down and reviewed on a regular basis, your subconscious mind can guide you in the right direction. Your subconscious mind, when driven by goals, will identify ideas and opportunities congruent with your goals. When you are driven by goals you will be more likely to see to completion the projects and tasks in line with your goals. Your subconscious mind will naturally get rid of tasks and projects not congruent with your goals.

Delegation is the next skill needed to help you tackle your to-do list. Whether you complete the task or you find the right person to complete it for you doesn't matter. The natural high and momentum are still yours! When you find someone else to complete a task for you, your goal is to get it done better or at least close to as good as you would have done it yourself. The beauty of delegation is that you are free to do other things while some of your important tasks are being completed.

The reality is not everything can be outsourced. Various tasks and projects still have to be done by you.

If there is anything in your life nagging you to be completed, decide whether the nagging is justified. If so, get the job done. Otherwise, cross it off the list and say "Next!"

Chapter 27

Laws For Accepting And Turning Down Opportunities

"Success breeds an increasing number of new opportunities" (Dan Kennedy)

Not heeding this wisdom can destroy your forward motion fast. I know - it happened to me!

You only have so much time and so many resources to accomplish what you are aiming for. Naturally, it is important to explore opportunity. The smell of opportunity certainly hits you on an emotional level. It is easy to be lured in a new direction with the promise of fulfilling a certain desire. How do you know if you should go for the opportunity?

The answer is in your "Opportunities Rulebook." You really don't need a book to do this. This "rule book" can live in your mind or, as you will see in a minute, on a sheet of paper. It starts with knowing what you don't want in your life. That's right, what you don't want! You will often realize after you've taken on a new opportunity you want the outcome, but not the necessary steps to the outcome.

Let's use a simple example. You're exploring ways to earn some extra money and purchased a course on real estate investing. You know most wealthy people have a certain amount of real estate, usually the kind that produces "positive cash flow." You know real estate can be a great vehicle for creating wealth and "passive income." This is the outcome you want.

Everything comes with a price. Therefore, to achieve this outcome you will have to invest in your education. Then you may have to deal with tenants, screen tenants, know how to inspect properties, spend time locating properties and higher people to make repairs. You must be willing to accept those facts if you are to achieve the outcome you desire. The point is this: All things have a price and you must be willing to pay the price to achieve the outcome the opportunity presents.

Let's start with your rulebook. This is fun and simple...

Take a second and list any circumstances or situations you do not want in your life. This list should also include activities you will not do under any circumstances. This may sound ridiculous, but if you don't want to do yard work, you don't have to. You can hire someone to do it or move into a condo! Think about the "don't wants" in your business and career - list them too.

When you are through with your "don't want list," move on to your "do want list." This is not merely a "wish list." Make it realistic. How do you want your day-to-day life to unfold? The list will be made up of the activities you are willing to do and look forward to doing on your way to achieving the outcomes you want.

You must be totally clear and honest with yourself. Remember opportunities really are simply a promise of a future outcome. To achieve any outcome, there must first be steps taken to produce it. Sometimes new opportunities require you to change direction and get in motion almost 180 degrees from where you currently are. Not every opportunity that comes along (and there will be plenty) will be right for you. If an opportunity comes along fits into your rules for accepting it, then go for it. This means you'll enjoy or at least be proficient at the activities that accompany the opportunity. It means these steps will be welcomed into your life. If an opportunity comes along and it's not conducive to what you want in your life, than you must stay away.

Be Really Careful With Your Signature

When the real estate bubble was in full swing, sometimes all it took was a signature for someone to move into the house of his dreams. If the house of his dreams proved to be unaffordable because of a sudden drop in income or a sudden jump in the mortgage payment, his signature quickly lost its value. Many would-be "real estate investors" have gone down the tubes by over-leveraging themselves via their personal signature. I was actually shocked when one morning on Fox News, I heard "The Donald" himself (that's Donald Trump) was being harassed by a lender who was demanding he own up to the huge (for most people) personal guarantee on one of his losing projects.

When times are good, it is easy to get lulled into freely signing your name to scary documents without reading the fine print. Worse, it's also easy to misjudge someone and lend them your signature. It's funny because both Jamie and I learned this the hard way.

Back in the days when we were dating, Jamie was almost $15,000 in credit card debt. A small portion of it was hers. She accumulated the debt when, after the 9/11 tragedy, the company she worked for in New York City went under due to the ripple effect of the terrorist attacks. It took her a little longer than she expected to find another job and in the process, she ran up a couple of thousand dollars on her credit card.

The rest of the debt was there because she freely gave her mother use of the credit line. This irresponsible action (on the part of Jamie) combined with actually trying to also pay her mother's gambling debts left her stuck with the bill. When we got married, we bought a house in Philadelphia and our mortgage was as much as Jamie's rent was in North Jersey. Our dual incomes but not dual expenses combined with Jamie landing a very good job in South Jersey helped us pay the debts off in no time at all. The lesson here - never co-sign for anyone! There are exceptions. I actually signed for a car for my brother after he got himself on his feet. However, I knew in my mind that if he couldn't pay for it – the car was mine. Therefore, I never worried about him not making the payments because frankly, if he didn't he'd be walking and I'd simply have two cars to choose from. But I made that decision before I co-signed for the car.

Another time when I freely signed my name, I was not as fortunate. When I sold one of my businesses there was some leased equipment. The lease had about eighteen months left on it. I tried like crazy to get the leasing company to take my name off as the personal guarantor, but they weren't having it. Then, you guessed it, when the new owner just couldn't make the business work due to poor management, apathy and the fact he had been in financial hot water since kindergarten, I had to pay the bill and deal with the headaches of trying to get the equipment which was rightfully mine.

Be careful with your signature whether you have great credit, good credit, or don't give a damn about your credit. It is better not to have to show up in court or screen all of your phone calls.

When New Opportunities Show Up In Your Personal Life, Choose Wisely

Have you ever heard of someone getting "cold feet" on their wedding day? It is a safe bet it was caused by the feeling of giving up on future "new opportunities" for love and romance. The natural human tendency of wanting what we can't have and under-appreciating what we do have helps a lot of therapist stay in business.

Time and circumstances always change. Therefore, life will always throws new opportunities in your path. Let's play a little game. Let's imagine right now that you are a single person with no children. The total opposite would be if you were married with a couple of kids.

When you get married and have kids, you realize you are basically starting a new life. The life of a single person requires you to take care of, usually, one person - you. When you are married with children and want to be the best spouse and parent you can be, it is now about you and your family. You'll maintain your unique identity, but you are now part of this one body that makes up your family. Marriage and family can be a wonderful thing for those who can make the transition from "just me" to "us and me." It is not easy!

The high divorce rate is an obvious sign many people thought they knew what they wanted. Translated - "I don't want to pass up this opportunity because I think it'll make me happy." However, it only makes sense to draw the conclusion people who end up divorced do so because they want "another opportunity." Or, they realized the opportunity of marriage to a particular person just wasn't what they wanted after all. It's not my place to judge; I'm just saying be careful! If a married couple is not happy then they have to take some sort of action. Life is too short.

I'd Like A Refund Please!

On my wedding day, my best man really made me laugh. He said, "If you and Jamie end up divorced I want a refund!" He was referring to a refund of the $500 cash wedding gift he gave us. About a year later, one of Jamie's friends got married. Naturally, Jamie was in the wedding party. Her friend married her "on again, off again" boyfriend of many years. She worked as a massage therapist and he worked as a physical therapist - a good match I guess? She had always been sort of quiet in social circles and he had always been a "party type." Well, less than a year, a new condo and a dog later they were divorced. He claimed she really had no clue what she wanted to do with her life and she claimed he just did not want to give up the "single life." I jokingly asked Jamie if we could have a refund! Not all was lost though. A less fortunate girl at the local high school ended up with a nice prom dress out of the deal.

I am not saying that all decisions should be irreversible. But if you treat them as if they are irreversible, it will force you to make a better decision. Add the discipline to turn to your "rulebook," and you'll end up making better decisions and not being so free with your "yeses."

Having a "New Opportunities Rulebook" will keep you sane by allowing your logic to work with your emotions to justify embracing or turning down opportunities in your personal or business life. The rulebook will also contribute to your overall happiness.

Missing Out

Did you know that a major cause of stress and unhappiness is the feeling that you are "missing out" on things? Many marketers use this truth to their advantage to sell you things you don't need or have no use for. Another source of stress and unhappiness is the natural regret of making bad decisions. Your rulebook is one key to your happiness because you'll sleep well at night knowing you've made a good decision to embrace or decline an opportunity.

Do You Ever Try Anything?

The answer to the question is NO. You're either going to do something or you're not. Unfortunately, the words "try" or "the act of trying" somehow gives people a middle ground. Trying is very casual. "I'll give this a try, and I'll give that a try, and if it doesn't work out, I can always go try something else." Terrible mentality!

Great marketers know all too well how to use "trying" to their advantage. Instead of asking you to buy their products, they'll let you "try it." And if you're not happy you can always send it back. People who are not schooled in marketing think that the sellers put themselves at risk by doing this. Actually, quite the opposite is true. If they don't give you that strong "try it before you buy it offer," their sales would suffer. Marketers know the word "try" is associated with being "noncommittal." The association between trying and being noncommittal is where the danger lies.

I was listening to a wonderful mp3 that I downloaded from one of the "guru's" Websites. The sixty-minute audio was really informative and inspirational. I've listened to it several times and every time I listened I learned something. But the guru said one thing on the recording that was totally wrong. At the end of the presentation he told the audience, "Now that you know the steps and the principles you can be successful in anything you pick. It doesn't matter what you pick – network marketing, the Internet, real estate, the principles are the same." The major point I did not agree with is when this guru said, "It doesn't matter what you pick." The fact is, it matters a lot! If you are not totally jazzed and fired up about what you do, you cannot be successful. Even if you make a ton of money doing it you are still not successful because you would still be searching for what does fire you up.

I have "tried" some different businesses. And I even applied "correct success principles" to them. I'll tell you the ones I have "tried" were huge time and money suckers. Of course, I did learn some things and skills from a few of them along the way, so not all was lost. But one valuable piece of wisdom I have learned over the years is to "TRY less and DO more."

There are reasons some activities in life hold your attention and get your passion going and others don't. Usually, the things in life that get you excited are the ones you have some sort of natural talent or gift for performing. It's these activities that deserve your attention. When you give these activities, ideas and ventures your attention, you will find your "trying" soon turns into succeeding.

Trying and not succeeding at too many different activities will eventually burn you out. Thomas Edison tried and failed 10,000 times with the electric light bulb, but that is what makes his trying the kind of trying that you want to embrace. Edison was an inventor who tried and failed at experiments that he was passionate about. He didn't fail at trying to invent the electric light bulb and then move on to the telephone, then fail trying to invent the telephone and move on to the television. He never would have invented anything if that were his M.O. He knew the light bulb was possible and was determined to make it work. His trials were tied to his passions and goals. (Passion plus Profit!)

One time, I "tried" learning how to trade stocks on my own. I lost $20,000 in two months! Hey, I tried! The truth is that opportunities to "try" new things are never in short supply and you really have to be careful what you try. So here's how you can judge whether you should give something a try or not...

I don't care how much money you can make if you try and succeed at this new (insert whatever). If you are not excited and passionate about it, it won't work. Think about this: Some media and politicians like to punish those who have become rich and powerful. They talk about greed and stepping on little people to get ahead. What many do not understand is that it is not money alone that drives some of the most financially successful people in the world. Warren Buffet, Oprah Winfrey, Bill Gates and even Donald Trump (as flashy as he is) are driven by way more than solely the need and desire for more money. I remember watching an episode of *The*

Apprentice, with Donald Trump when he said, "I like buildings." You can't get any simpler than that - the guy likes buildings and guess what he does ... he builds buildings!

So what is it that you like? I am not talking about watching football or going to play cards with your friends. I'm talking about what drives you? What do you really want to contribute to the world? It is the answers to those questions that will determine what you should be "trying." My rule is that I only try things that are totally related to my publishing and consulting business. For example, I learned how to practice hypnosis for a few very good reasons; it is an outgrowth of my natural talent for helping people. Since I help other businesses sell and market, and hypnosis deals with the subconscious, it is certainly another "ace" up my sleeve. Plus, hypnosis just kept coming up over and over again in different people that I have looked up to over the years. Joe Vitale's involvement with hypnosis is what pushed me over the edge after I read two of his books: *Hypnotic Writing* and *There's A Customer Born Every Minute*. My fascination finally took over so I sought out a teacher and learned how to do it. It had little to do with "how much money I can make" as a hypnotist. In fact, I really don't practice that much on others, but at least I pursued my interest and it has helped me.

When you "try" things that are in line with your goals you are not really "trying." You are succeeding even if you don't succeed! When you "try" things that you are not passionate about or have no interest in other than financial gain, most of your trials will end up as failures. And as a result, you'll end up a step away from your goals.

Remember the "4 P's"

Apply Proven Principles to your Passion and Purpose

Chapter 28

Principles To Live By

"I demand more from myself than anybody else could ever expect" (Anthony Robbins)

There are laws that govern our society for our protection. There are laws that govern the universe. It is crucial for you to create your own personal laws and principles to live by too. Yes, they must adhere to the laws of society, and they certainly must not violate the laws of the universe.

To "go with the flow" is not always the best method. Simply reacting in a "knee-jerk" way to life can do a lot of harm. Having a guiding set of principles to follow in your personal or business life will protect you from unfavorable people and situations.

For example, if a business owner has certain rules that govern the interactions with his customers, these are the principles of his business. Therefore, he would be very clear with any employees about adopting these principles during work hours. If someone seeks a job with him, they must follow these principles too.

Perhaps you want to live by the principle of professional excellence in your chosen field. If so, you would always meet deadlines, return phone calls and do your best to offer service that is above and beyond the call of duty or what is expected.

And Then They Will Complain About The Recession

Jamie and I like to have someone come in and clean our home for us every two weeks or so. About three months after moving into our new home, I went online and found a cleaning service. They came about three times and did a pretty good job. I called them to schedule again like I had the previous times. That was the turning point, because they never showed up to do the job. At first I was forgiving, but after four times of scheduling and not showing, I had enough! I called two other services. One actually showed but did a less than professional job. The other missed the very first appointment we made and then didn't bother taking the initiative to call back and reschedule.

I was ready to give up and get my cleaning

clothes on when I came across a small ad in the local paper for a cleaning service. Rebecca was nice, professional and prompt. She actually charges less to clean our house compared to the other three. She has never missed an appointed time and actually showed up once after a bad ice storm! The point is Rebecca obviously adheres to certain principles of excellence. You might say, "Come on, she is only cleaning houses." In every field, every business and every company most people are just "average." That is why when you follow certain principles you easily stand out! In my corporate training programs and small business consulting, programs my main focus is to help the company and individuals stand out by learning and practicing the behaviors of excellence. The funny thing is that the same people and businesses that constantly perform poorly are the first to complain about how unfair life is or how bad the economy is.

Personal Principles

Personal principles are slightly different for everyone. I will not suggest to you a list of "personal principles" that I believe you should live by. Not my concern.

Here's why I won't "suggest" principles to you...

Throughout this book, I have related personal stories and the many lessons learned from them. I am offering you a buffet of principles you can apply to your success as you see fit. It is very dangerous to impose your personal principles on other people.

One of the principles I adhere to is constant learning. I read and listen to informational programs daily. I teach this principle to my children. I recommend it to my clients and require it of anyone I employ. But I will not force my spouse, neighbors, friends, or relatives to do the same. "Mind your own business!" It is no part of your mission in life to correct people's morals, habits, practices, or principles. And if their chosen principles are affecting you, get them out of your life. Remember – the choice is yours, use your influence to help people who want to be helped.

It is more important to your success that you allow certain principles to govern your life as you see fit. Occasional instances will no doubt call for some flexibility, but most will not. For example, if you highly value the time you spend with your children or significant other, you will not easily let another individual take that time from you. You will kindly request to schedule another time to discuss the matter. However, if you have a tremendous opportunity that relates to an important goal in your life you've been working on and it happens to conflict with your "family time," you would probably make an exception and not feel bad about it. Your family wouldn't either.

Positive "Exceptions" Are Good, Negative "Exceptions" Are Bad

I learned from Brian Tracy that there is really NO middle ground. You're either engaging in behaviors that bring you closer to your goals, or your behaviors are bringing you away from your goals. If you have decided you are going to achieve your ideal weight and fitness level, then you basically have decided to live by certain principles. You'll eat healthy foods, you'll be sure that most or all of your food has been grown in the earth and not manufactured somewhere. You'll exercise daily or several times per week. These are now your basic guiding principles. It would be a good idea for you to build in some flexibility too. Maybe you'll eat dessert on the weekends or have a beer or two. But during the week, you are committed to remaining congruent with your principles of healthy eating. If you make an exception by eating dessert on Thursday, it is easy to justify it by saying, "That's OK! I'll just skip dessert on Saturday to balance things out." You are setting yourself up for failure and disappointment!

It is much easier to stay congruent with your principles than make up for them by compensating somewhere else. If you make a commitment to read good books like this one for thirty minutes daily, that is a principle that will help you enormously with your success. However, if you decide to watch TV rather than do your reading, and justify it by telling yourself that you will read an hour tomorrow, you are making a negative exception. Negative exceptions to your principles will undermine your success. The alcoholic who has been sober for years cannot just have one drink. The hardcore drug addict cannot simply just smoke weed.

My negative behaviors and your negative behaviors are linked to other behaviors. Remember when I say "negative behaviors," I am talking about any behaviors that detract from your goals. The person who recently quits smoking must avoid drinking too much alcohol because in the past, he'd smoke and drink at the same time. For a while, I battled with allowing email to distract my creative time. I'd be working on my writing and have my email up in another window on my laptop. The positive behavior and principle I chose to live by in my life was to be more productive and make every minute of my day count.

Writing takes a lot of focus, and the truth is that I am able to produce much better work if I am not distracted. I also had to balance this principle with my principle of high levels of service and responsiveness to my most valued clients. The happy balance was to not pull up my email until a certain time each day. I posted the hours that I would be available via email and everyone was happy - My clients, my readers and me!

When you look to do away with a negative behavior, you must also address other behaviors in the process. For example, a lot of people eat because they are bored, stressed or emotionally down. If they would just do away with eating for the wrong reasons, they would be at their ideal weight. If they go for a walk instead of eating, that would be helpful and better stress management in the long run. The other problem with eating for the wrong reasons is that most of the time the food that's available is less than healthy. People who are stressed and subconsciously want to eat are not going to prepare a healthy meal; they are going to reach for whatever is easy. I'm just using the eating thing as an example, but keeping an eye on "linked behaviors" can help you move toward your goals faster.

What About Positive Exceptions?

As I have stated above, I think that positive exceptions are good. Positive exceptions are exceptions that can shortcut your progress. They are exceptions that will get you closer to your goals. The key is to recognize them and act on them. Positive exceptions can sometimes take you out of your comfort zone, and that is fine. It is outside of the comfort zone where we achieve the most! Positive exceptions are sometimes pointed out to us by others. "I never looked at it that way – I think you're right" can be words associated with a positive exception to your principles. There is this saying that tradition is the enemy of progress and progress is the enemy of tradition.

Take some time to think about which principles you want guiding your life. A set of guiding principles can help you make decisions, set goals and design a life that you want. As long as your principles don't violate the laws of society, the laws of the universe or bring on unnecessary heartache to those around you, you'll be fine. If you are married or in a serious relationship, it would be a good idea to get the people closest to you involved in your guiding principles.

Chapter 29

Words Of Wisdom On Finishing Strong

"Each time I find myself lying flat on my face I just pick myself up and get back in the race."

I love when Frank Sinatra sings that line in his hit song *That's Life*.

The truth is you will get bumped around and knocked down. Someone will not always be there to pick you up, and you'll have to pick yourself up and get back in the race.

"Lie down with dogs, wake up with fleas"

You'll come across your share of shady people that will step on you to get ahead. These people are just out to grab as much as they can. They simply have scarcity mentalities. They believe that in order to get a bigger slice of the pie they must take yours. Expanding the pie for everyone or "baking more pies" is not an option for them. Fortunately for you and me, this tactic seldom works. When it does work its success is usually short-lived. A quick personal example...

When I moved, I planned on selling the business I owned in my previous town. The best candidate was the person who was running it in my absence. In a few short months, I had done my very best to teach this individual the ins and outs of running a profitable business. It was really just a matter of time before I felt confident that he could do it totally without my guidance and off-site management. An owner has to deal with much more than an employee. There is a huge leap that has to be made in order to go from employee to owner.

His repayment to me was to leave abruptly and to tell numerous clients that "this place is closing because I am leaving." His goal was to simply take the clients to his own location. I totally blame myself for this debacle, and I should have seen it coming. The funny thing was that his plan did not really go as he expected. I saved the business and found someone (actually he found me) to take it over. The guy I found was no angel either but living seven hours away (by car), I really did not have many options. The guy who left abruptly was simply driven by the greed that many employees, especially of small entrepreneurial businesses, are overcome by when they only see one side of the coin. I don't hold any animosity toward this guy, and I wish him the best. The world is really abundant! The funny thing was a year later, I heard through the grapevine that he was making less money than he was when he worked for me. Idiot!

Two lessons I learned from the experience

Guys! If you are married, trust your wife's ability to judge people. I hired the man who attempted to shut my business down way too fast. My wife told me to take my time and keep looking for the right person. If you are not married, have perspective business associates meet your mother! Bottom line, have someone in your life that can help you judge the people you are about to associate with.

"It's not where you start in life, it's where you finish that really counts"

Bob Alexander also told me, "It's not where you start in life, it's where you finish that matters." Most of the wealthiest people in the world came from very humble beginnings. Oprah Winfrey and Bill Clinton come to mind as two very well-known people who started with the odds stacked against them. Many non-famous owners of successful companies started from scratch and overcame enormous adversity to get to where they are. Where will you finish? I know you'll finish wherever you determine is a success for you.

"You're better off finishing with an unfinished list"

Keep in mind what I am about to tell you is not contrary to what I said earlier about unfinished tasks. Unfinished tasks are fine if you are working on finishing them. Picture yourself driving down the road in a rural area; I don't want to stereotype but there are places where extra cars just seem to pile up on private property. Some of these cars look like they are being worked on by the owner. Maybe his hobby is to fix them up. His UN-finished tasks are OK because his joy comes from tinkering around. Then, there's always the person who is meaning to restore that old car that's on his land, but just never does. It sits there year after year and he never tinkers with it. Finally, someone from the Town's Zoning or Planning Board gets fed up with the complaints and orders the vehicle removed. I have a license to write the words above because I live in New Hampshire.

The guy who was tinkering is better off because at least he took action. The guy who just let the car sit there never took action. When your time comes to leave planet Earth, let it be with a to-do list of items you're working on and want to get done. This is NOT a bad thing! Success requires motion, and an object in motion will continue to stay in motion. Stay in motion until the day you die! It is okay if your "bucket list" expands.

***

Evergreen Success Principle

By The Yard It's Hard, But Inch By Inch, Anything's A Cinch

Keep the big picture in mind at all times, but remember success is a result of many little things done right over a period of time. If you are getting things done every day that move you toward your goals, you are living the life you want. Your larger goal will be realized. It is just a matter of time! The world is often misled by the "overnight" success story. What they fail to report in those stories is the time, effort and "backstage preparation" that went into the success. Work hard every day toward your goals, and just like hitting the "Total" button on a cash register, your little accomplishments will add up to your total success!

***

Chapter 30

What Would Your Friends Ask You If They Found Out You Recently Ran In A Marathon?

"Success seems to be a matter of holding on after others have let go" (William Feather)

I interviewed a guy named, Warren Greshes for a program I worked on a few years ago. Warren wrote a book called *The Best Damn Sales Book Ever* ... I know ... interesting title for a book. Anyway, Warren related to me that when someone runs in a marathon they are asked a different question than if they competed in a sprint or a 100-yard dash. He said; "If you compete in a sprint or dash, people are interested in whether you win or not. But when you run in a marathon, they're curious not so much of you coming out first, but whether you actually complete the race. Everyone knows that the winner is always a guy from Kenya!"

Life is a marathon! It only matters that you finish. You have to define "finish." I think the best way to define finish is to constantly work toward worthwhile goals - goals that help you and in the process of helping you, help others. If I succeeded in helping you get in motion to reach your goals, then I'd consider my work here a success.

It has been a pleasure helping you get things in motion in your life.

Do it Now

W. Clement Stone built a fortune from scratch in the insurance business. He was famous for brainwashing his salesmen with the saying, "Do it now." He knew there was usually no better time to get started then now! The lights won't always be on green. Get in motion and Do It NOW!

Please do stay in touch! Visit some of my Websites (I have listed them on the following pages) and subscribe to my free e-newsletter. If you'd like to have me speak to a group of business people, salespeople, association or any community organization, I am happy and passionate about sharing the Success Secret That Never Fails with your group!

All the best!

Mike D.
Mike@AskMikeD.com
www.askmiked.com

Resources Available To You From The Author

<u>Bring Mike D. in to Speak for Your Group!</u>
Mike D. can speak for your club, company or organization. Whether you are looking for a keynote presentation, a breakout session or a workshop, Mike can be the ideal speaker for your next event or meeting. Mike is not a "Motivational Speaker" - he is the world's only "Mobilizational Speaker," because it is all about action! Here's a partial list of his presentations. For updated info visit: www.AskMikeD.com/services/speaking

"The Success Secret That Never Fails"

In this keynote or breakout session, Mike will cover the key points that your audience needs to get in motion and make things happen quickly. This talk will inspire them to get into action so they can reach team and personal goals.

"Magic Words That Bring You Clients and Customers"

This talk is ideal for marketers, salespeople, business owners and anyone whose results are tied to the cooperation of others. Mike will cover Persuasion Secrets of the Written and Spoken Word so your audience can immediately go out and start selling more effectively.

"Internet & Mobile Marketing Secrets for Your Business"

Online lead generation, successful internet marketing strategies, mobile marketing and getting your best prospects to go "from cyberspace to your place" is this focus of this program.

"7 Ways to Get Your Business and Personal Life Moving"

The title of this talk pretty much sums it up!

For queries and questions regarding availability, please send an email to Mike@AskMikeD.com or call 267.992.2970

Website Design, Copywriting, Online and Offline Marketing Consulting and Business Strategy

If you are looking for fresh ideas and insights to propel your business forward, then this program may be for you. Mike will help you design and implement marketing campaigns and strategies. Mike will help you turn the features of your business into irresistible benefits that your ideal customers will be attracted to. Mike will help you uncover the buried treasure in your current business and open up new opportunities and income streams that you've been overlooking. Mike's team can design a website for you that is found by your best prospects and quickly turns them into clients.

Visit: CyberspaceToYourPlace.com

About the Author

Mike Dolpies (AKA Mike D.) is a Veteran Small Business Owner, Consultant and Speaker. He started his first business just six months out of high school at the age of eighteen. He speaks for corporations and associations on the topics of Success, Peak Performance, Publicity, Mobile Marketing and Ethical Persuasion. Mike's practical and entertaining advice is based on his years of real world experience and his constant and never-ending learning. He can be reached at www.cyberspacetoyourplace.com or www.askmiked.com

The Best Quote You'll Ever Read...

"They Say a Picture is Worth a Thousand Words. But Did You Know an Action is Worth a Thousand Pictures? So an Action is Worth a Million Words."

Like Quotes?

Get some of Mike D's Original Quotes At... http://www.askmiked.com/about-us/quotes-by-mike-d/

22937621R00126

Made in the USA
Lexington, KY
20 May 2013